One
Big
Beautiful
Bead

One Big Beautiful Bead

Simple Jewelry with Focal Beads

Sarah McConnell

LARK BOOKS

A Division of Sterling Publishing Co., Inc.
New York / London

Editor: Jean Campbell

Art Director: Kathleen Holmes

Cover Designer: Cindy LaBreacht

Assistant Editor: Shannon P. Quinn-Tucker

Associate Art Director: Shannon Yokeley

Art Production Assistant: Jeff Hamilton

Editorial Assistance: Mark Bloom
Cassie Moore

Art Intern: Michael Foreman

Illustrators: Bernie Wolf
Lance Wille
Shannon Yokeley

Photographer: Stewart O'Shields

Library of Congress Cataloging-in-Publication Data

McConnell, Sarah.
    One big beautiful bead : simple jewelry with focal beads / Sarah McConnell.—1st ed.
        p. cm.
    Includes index. 37648416   6/08
    ISBN-13: 978-1-60059-064-1 (hc-plc with jacket : alk. paper)
    ISBN-10: 1-60059-064-0 (hc-plc with jacket : alk. paper)
    1. Beadwork   2. Jewelry making.   I. Title.
TT860.B33385 2004
745.594'2—dc22

                                2007015982

10 9 8 7 6 5 4 3 2 1

First Edition

Published by Lark Books, A Division of Sterling Publishing Co., Inc., 387 Park Avenue South, New York, N.Y. 10016

Text © 2007, Sarah McConnell
Photography © 2007, Lark Books unless otherwise specified
Illustrations © 2007, Lark Books unless otherwise specified

Distributed in Canada by Sterling Publishing, c/o Canadian Manda Group, 165 Dufferin Street, Toronto, Ontario, Canada M6K 3H6

Distributed in the United Kingdom by GMC Distribution Services,

Castle Place, 166 High Street, Lewes, East Sussex, England BN7 1XU

Distributed in Australia by Capricorn Link (Australia) Pty Ltd., P.O. Box 704, Windsor, NSW 2756 Australia

If you have questions or comments about this book, please contact:

Lark Books
67 Broadway
Asheville, NC 28801
(828) 253-0467

Manufactured in China

ISBN 13: 978-1-60059-064-1
ISBN 10: 1-60059-064-0

For information about custom editions, special sales, premium and corporate purchases, please contact Sterling Special Sales Department at 800-805-5489 or specialsales@sterlingpub.com.

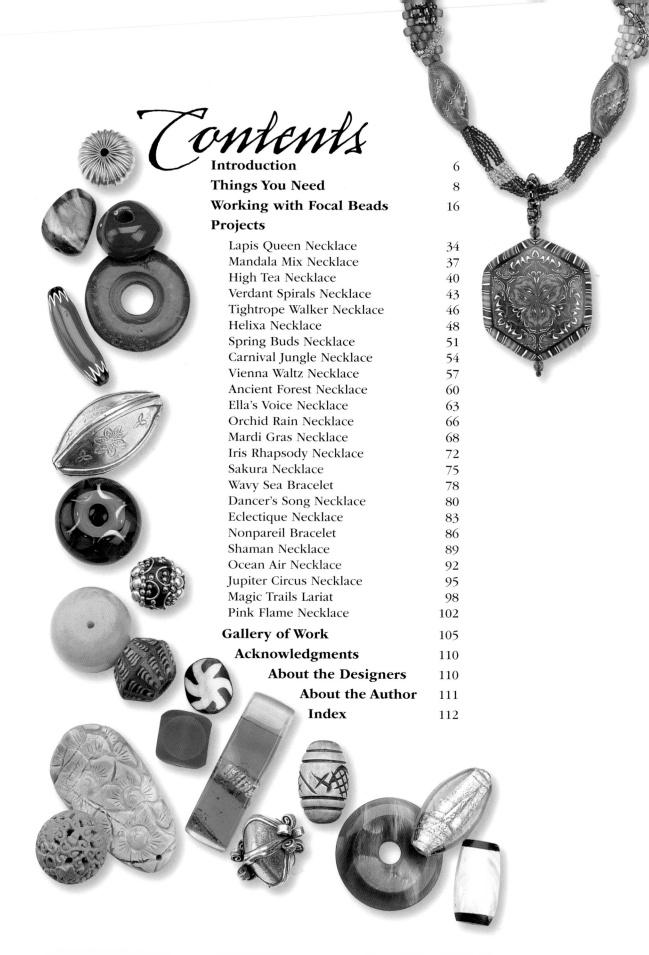

Contents

Sarah McConnell
Coral Sea, 2004
Focal bead by Karen Ovington
21½ inches (54.6 cm)
Etched focal bead, seed beads, sterling silver
Photo by Robert McConnell

Introduction

What exactly is a focal bead, and what's so great about it? A focal bead is the centerpiece, or focal point, of a piece of jewelry you design. Focal beads can range from relatively small to fearsomely large and are made from pretty much anything you can think of—glass, metal, stone, wood, bone, shell, and polymer clay.

Okay, what's so great about a big bead, besides the fact you can actually find it if you drop it down the back of the sofa? Inspiration, that's what. I tried all sorts of arts and crafts, and the worst thing about all of them was staring at that big white piece of paper (or whatever) and having my mind go just as blank. What was I thinking? Why on earth did I think it would be fun to do some art?

This is where a big focal bead comes in. It's pretty, it has color and texture, and maybe even a theme. ("Hmmm ... I bet some nice porcelain beads would go with this focal bead that looks like a ki-mono.") If it's big enough, you've already got that part of your jew-elry design done as soon as you pick it up—how great is that? And now you've got something to design around. What colors to use? The bead is already telling you, and there's a whole section in this book (see page 16) devoted to what would look best. Or, if you've already done it before, there are some interesting things inside for you to try that you may not have done before.

Don't know anything about focal beads? It's all here. When I first got interested in focal beads, I took classes on how to make my own. What I learned from bead making is how much I appreciate focal beads as works of art. They are like little paintings I can hang around my neck. I can take this work of art with me instead of just hanging it up on a wall. Like a painting, a focal bead can tell me its own story. It might remind me of things I know, like the colors of spring and flowers in the garden. Or it can take me somewhere I've never been—to far-off Asia, a distant galaxy, or somewhere in between. I delight in each and every one of them. And when I find a wonderful focal bead, I now can look and think, "This would be great with crystals ... or a spiral rope ... or a peyote stitch." These beads truly serve up a delicious buffet of de-sign possibilities.

You can choose to simply slide a focal bead on a string. But if you've only worked with small beads in the past, focal beads can be a bit (or a lot) bigger and heavier than what you're used to. This book will teach you how to string them so you won't have to worry about the strand ever breaking. It will show you how to accent the focal bead and make it the showcase it deserves to be.

But there's more to focal beads than just stringing them. Maybe you've got a great big luscious focal bead, and you're thinking it would just look a little lonely on a string. Or maybe you want to make a fashion statement. This book will teach you how to string multiple strands, and when you're flush with success from doing that, you can move on to combining off-loom beadwork, or beadweaving, with your focal bead.

If you can string beads (and anyone can), you can beadweave. You can make a whole fabric of beads and use it to showcase your focal bead. This book shows you how to combine the very easiest stitches (like peyote stitch and spiral ropes) with your focal bead in a very secure and polished way.

When you pick up a focal bead, I would love for you to share my delight in that little work of art. I want you to be able to think of at least fifty exciting possibilities for it, be inspired as you start your design, watch it take on a life of its own, and then see how great your piece of jewelry turns out. And you will never, ever, lack for inspiration again ... it all starts with one big beautiful bead.

Top: Sarah McConnell
Gaia, 2002
Focal bead by Stevi Belle
18 inches (45.7 cm)
Focal bead, seed beads, quartz; simple spiral rope
Photo by Robert McConnell

Bottom: Sarah McConnell
Pink & Blue Spiral, 2006
Focal bead by Robert Jennik
18 inches (45.7 cm)
Focal bead, seed beads, freshwater pearls; simple spiral rope
Photo by Robert McConnell

Things You Need

When designing a piece of jewelry with a focal bead you never find yourself with a lack of inspiration. Just looking at one of these big beautiful beads can evoke memories, seasons, and textures. They can be elegant or exotic, simple or flashy. And as the designer, you get to decide how to bring out their charm—not a hard job, considering they seem to have limitless design potential. I often wish I could clone some of my favorites, so I could try all my different ideas.

Once you learn how to design around a focal bead, you can make beautiful pieces of jewelry unlike any others you've seen. You'll be surprised to learn how easy it is to work with these design gems, and how simple it is to make a piece that won't break, no matter how big the bead you are using. So, because you might be beading with a different animal than what you've beaded with before, carefully review the next sections of the book to learn the tricks, tips, and techniques I've discovered on my odyssey beading these big bold beads.

Materials

The materials you'll use for the projects in this book are beads; something to string them on; and the metal components (or "findings") to put them all together. The goal is to make something that you'll admire now and for years to come, so be sure to buy the best materials possible.

Beads

Beads come in such a wide variety of types, colors, and shapes, there isn't a book large enough to list them all. The following outlines the beads featured in this book and can set you on your way to discovering your own treasure trove of beads.

Focal Beads

One good way to learn more about focal beads is to visit your local bead shop. Walk all the way through the store without buying anything. Note the prices and sizes of the focal beads that interest you. After a quick spin, you'll get a sense of which beads attract you, and you'll probably have a healthy shopping list—focal beads are that alluring.

Because focal beads are bigger, and often heavier, than their smaller counterparts, you need to carefully consider how to incorporate them into your jewelry designs. Necklaces, bracelets, and earrings need to be designed in a way so the bead hangs in a delicate balance with the rest of the piece's materials. It's also important to consider the bead's weight. If it's very heavy, you need to make sure the focal bead doesn't stress the piece overall, slowly pulling the piece apart.

Please see pages 14, 19, 22, 29, and 31 to learn even more about these beauties—you're bound to be inspired!

Accent Beads

Accent bead is the term I use for beads used to separate the focal bead from seed beads, or to separate one section of a jewelry design from another. There are dozens and dozens of types, but a list of my favorites follows.

Crystal beads are available in many lovely colors and shapes. Austrian crystals are generally considered to be the highest quality. When you use crystal beads, keep in mind that their holes have rough edges that can cut thread. If you find a piece breaking suddenly, a crystal bead may be the culprit. A remedy to this is to make sure you have a seed bead strung at each end of the crystal bead.

Freshwater pearls also make great accent beads. They come in many different shapes and colors. Pearls have very small holes, so if you use them, plan on only being able to make one or two thread passes, or using very thin flexible beading wire.

Metal beads make terrific accent beads. They come in all kinds of metal, including sterling silver, fine silver, gold-filled, brass, and copper. When purchasing metal beads, it's important to consider how the piece will be worn—if it's something that will be worn often, for example, you'll want to be sure the bead's finish is durable and not overly prone to tarnish.

Pressed-glass beads make pretty accent beads. They are made from hot glass poured into a mold, cooled, tumbled, and then sometimes covered with a finish. They come in a vast amount of shapes, including melons, flowers, and leaves.

Suzanna Biro
Untitled, 2006
Length: 22 inches (55.9 cm)
Fine silver, amber, black jasper, dZi beads; stringing
Photo by Stewart O'Shields

Seed Beads

Seed beads, another type of bead you'll use for many of the projects in this book, are tiny glass beads. They come in a variety of shapes such as round, hexagonal ("hex"), cube, and triangular. The largest used in this book is size 2°, the smallest is size 11° (with seed beads, a smaller number means a bigger size). They come in a wide array of colors and finishes.

Tips

Use a needle threader to make threading the small eyes of beading needles easier; the extra-small kind used by fly fishermen to tie flies work best.

Stringing Materials

The projects in this book use three types of stringing materials: beading thread, flexible beading wire, and metal wire. In each case, use the highest quality you can afford. Since these materials are what keep your design in one piece, you want to make sure your creation stays in one piece for years to come.

Beading thread is a nylon thread that feels much like silk. It comes in dozens of colors. Some beading threads come pre-waxed, but if yours doesn't, coat it liberally with wax or thread conditioner.

Flexible beading wire is created by twisting many minutely-thin stainless steel strands together and sealing the bundle with a nylon coating. It's a very strong stringing material and the types with higher strand counts have a surprisingly gentle drape. Beading wire is

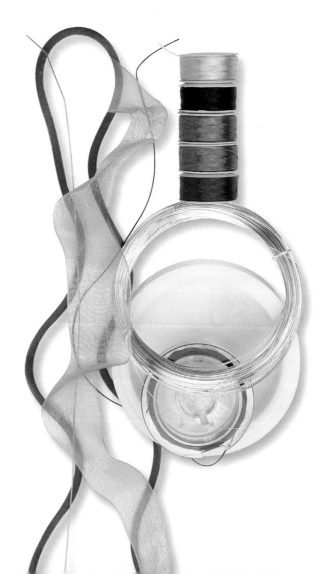

Tips

Sterling silver wire is bound to tarnish. But if you don't have a polishing cloth handy, just put some dry kitchen baking soda on your fingers and rub the wire with your fingers. Then wipe off the wire with a soft cloth and it will shine like new.

available in many different sizes. The medium-width (.019 inch [.48 mm]) wire works well for most projects, but if you're using pearls, the fine (.014 inch [.36 mm]) or very fine (.010 inch [.25 mm]) widths might be a better choice. *Note*: To secure beading wire, use special knots (see Knots, page 25) or crimp beads (see Crimping wire, page 21).

Metal wire is mainly used in this book for forming wireworked loops and stringing cones. It comes in a range of thicknesses, but 20- to 22-gauge (the smaller the number, the thicker the wire) are the sizes used in this book. You can purchase all types of metal wire, but the most common ones used to make fine beaded jewelry are sterling silver- and gold-filled.

Sheer fabric ribbon is a unique way to string light focal beads. Organza works very well because it can pass through relatively small bead holes.

Silk cord is the traditional material for stringing and knotting pearls, but it can be used to string other types of beads, too. It lends a beautiful drape and comes in an array of colors and thicknesses.

Jean Campbell
Rod Serling Couture, 2007
20 inches (50.8 cm)
Printed domino, coin charms, prayer wheels, brass milagro, sterling silver clasp with carnelian inset, found chain; stringing, wirework
Photo by Stewart O'Shields

Findings

The items you use to build your jewelry, such as clasps, cones, and headpins, are what beaders call *findings*. There are dozens of types, but the ones that follow are the most important for the projects in this book.

Clasps come in many varieties, including (top row, right to left) S and fishhook clasps, box clasps; (second row, right to left) magnetic clasps, buttons; (third row, right to left) lobster clasps, toggle clasps; (bottom) hook-and-eye clasps.

Bead caps are used to decoratively cover the ends of a bead.

Buttons can be used as closures on bracelets or necklaces. Using unique buttons can add a lot of character to a design.

Clasps connect the ends of a bracelet or necklace. There is a wide variety from which to choose. *Box clasps* have one half that's made up of a tiny hollow box. The other half is a tab that clicks into the box to lock the clasp. *Hook-and-eye clasps* consist of a fishhook shape with a loop at one end onto which you connect the wire or thread. The other side of the clasp is a soldered jump ring. *Lobster-claw clasps* are spring-activated clasps that are shaped like their namesake. Lock the clasp by attaching it to a soldered-closed jump ring. *S clasps* are shaped like the letter S. They have jump rings on each end to which you connect the ends of a piece. *Toggle clasps* have one side that's shaped

like a ring, the other like a bar. Once attached to the ends of a piece of jewelry, the bar slips through the ring vertically, and then moves horizontally across the ring to secure the piece.

Cones are cone-shaped findings used to hide the knots that secure a clasp to a multi-strand piece of jewelry.

Crimp beads and tubes are small cylinders of metal used to secure findings to beading wire. (See page 21 for instructions.)

Head pins are used to create bead dangles, like those in a pair of earrings. They are composed of a straight wire with a tiny disk or other design at one end to hold beads in place.

Jump rings are rounds of wire used to connect pieces of wire or findings. *Note*: Always open jump rings laterally using two chain-nose pliers (see figure 1). Never open them horizontally, or you'll weaken the wire.

Figure 1

Findings are the metal pieces that connect and finish jewelry designs. Shown is a selection that includes bead caps, cones, head pins, and jump rings.

Tools

The tools you'll use to make your focal bead jewelry are a matter of preference and budget. Some people are happy with a basic set of tools from a local hobby shop, while others want the best that money can buy. I purchased my first set at a department store, and though I bought higher-quality ones when I could justify it, I still use my original set. For the projects in this book, you'll need just a handful of tools.

Beading needles are thin wires with a tiny hole at one end. Size 10 and size 12 (the smaller the number, the larger the eye) work best for the projects featured in this book.

Beading mats or beading dishes help keep your beads organized and off the floor.

Clips are temporarily placed at the end of your stringing material to keep beads from sliding off the end. The toothless type used by electricians work very well for this purpose.

Jeweler's wire cutters have very sharp blades that come

A selection of pliers is an important addition to any beader's tool box: (from left) round-nose pliers, chain-nose pliers, crimping pliers (with crimping beads).

to a point. One side of the pliers leaves a V-shaped cut, the other side leaves a flat, or "flush," cut. Keep one pair of wire cutters for trimming precious metal wire. Use another one for cutting flexible beading wire, which will eventually dull the blade.

A measuring tape is helpful for figuring the lengths of wire for cutting, measuring findings and beads, and testing jewelry designs for fit.

Pliers are used to grasp and bend wire. *Chain-nose pliers* have jaws that are flat on the inside, and taper to a point on the outside. They are used for making sharp-angled bends. *Round-nose pliers* have rounded inside jaws that taper to a point on the outside. They are used for making loops. *Crimping pliers* are used for attaching crimp beads and crimp tubes to beading wire. (See page 21 for instructions on how to use crimping pliers.)

Scissors are used for cutting beading thread. Small, sharp, pointed embroidery scissors work especially well.

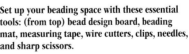

Set up your beading space with these essential tools: (from top) bead design board, beading mat, measuring tape, wire cutters, clips, needles, and sharp scissors.

Natural Material Focal Beads

Bone, horn, shell, stone, and wood beads were the very first type of beads ever created. These beads made from natural materials are easy to come by at most bead shops, are relatively inexpensive, and can be very intricate and artful.

Bone

Bone beads are created from the bones of working animals like camels, cows, goats, and yaks, but also from other animals like buffalo and antelope. They are relatively soft and are often carved into interesting shapes. They are porous, too, so the originally-white beads take dye very well. Bone focal beads are relatively light, so don't require much extra reinforcement when stringing. Choose the very finest bone focal beads—ones with no surface holes.

Horn

This type of bead is taken from many of the same animals that bone beads come from. Because they are made from horn instead of bones, they are harder and stronger, and have a natural shimmering quality. They are commonly available in red and brown tones, and have been traditionally used in ethnic-looking jewelry. Keep an open mind, however, because horn beads also look great paired with glass, silver, and other more contemporary beads. Find horn focal beads that have clean, even cuts with no chips or flaking.

Nut

Kukui, pelinut, edjok, betelnut, lumbang, tagua … these are all nuts, mainly from tropical regions, that can all be turned into beautiful focal beads. Sometimes they are dyed or painted, and some look best natural. Tagua nut focal beads have gained a huge popularity in the last several years. The nuts are harvested from the rainforest floor, and local artisans carve and paint them to create amazing results, often featuring Amazonian flowers and creatures.

Shell

Shell focal beads often feature the lustrous mother-of-pearl found in mollusks from around the world (mainly China and India). Each type of mollusk produces a different type of shell, so this kind of bead comes in a huge variety of colors and looks. They are cut in all sorts of shapes, but shell donuts and pendants are very popular. Some of the finest shell beads have etchings on them, lifting them to an artful new level.

Pearls

Pearls, while not considered to be shell beads, are formed inside mollusks (often oysters or clams). When its inner body becomes irritated by a foreign object or parasite, the mollusk forms a layer of mother-of-pearl around the object to protect itself, and will often continue to add enough layers to create a solid pearl. There are two types of pearls—ocean and freshwater. Ocean pearls are usually more uniform in shape, but tend to be very expensive. Freshwater pearls are easier to find, and come in a huge variety of colors and shapes. It's hard to find pearls large enough to qualify as focal beads, but occasionally you do. Just be wary of dyed freshwater pearls—the dye often comes off. Coral beads are not shell, either, but are oceanic in nature. They often are mistakenly lumped into the semi-precious stone category because they are extremely hard and often polished to a very high sheen. Coral beads are composed of the ectoskeletons of thousands of creatures who build towers of a hard rock-like substance. Red coral is in most demand, but is very hard to find, so be sure you know what you're paying for—many coral beads are dyed red, or are actually shell beads dyed red and sold as coral.

Stone

Focal beads are also made from every type of stone imaginable. The market demand for unusual semiprecious stones has become very strong, and some unique types of stone beads have made their way to bead and hobby shops, including amazonite, kyanite, and rutilated quartz, just to name a few. Most semiprecious stone focal beads are simply cut and polished and look great as is. Other times, the stones (especially soft ones like jade, serpentine, and agate) are intricately carved. There are also interesting etching and chemical dyeing techniques that lend another layer of interest to this type of bead. Stone beads are often heavy and should generally be strung on beading wire, not thread. Keep in mind that they are often rough on the inside, which is another good reason for stringing them on wire.

Wood

Wood is a very versatile material for bead making. It's easily carved, sanded, stamped, dyed, and painted, so you can find gorgeous wood focal beads on the market. They come in all sorts of woods, such as bayong, ebony, rosewood, and sandalwood. It's more typical to find small wood beads, but if you look hard, you'll be able to find focal-bead sizes as well. When buying, check for any splitting at the grain, surface chips, or other possible problems.

The first focal beads ever made were created from natural materials, but the beads of today have changed quite a bit from those first adornments. Shown here, a beautiful variety of types including horn, bone, shell, nut, and wood.

Working with Focal Beads

Once you've got all your materials and tools gathered, you're ready to take the next step in putting together a fantastic piece of jewelry. If you haven't done it before, it can be intimidating to design with one big beautiful bead, but just think—the bigger the bead, the closer you are to a finished project! Not only is size a plus in working with these beauties, but a focal bead also lends a great place to start the design process itself. By just looking at the bead, you can get a sense of which colors you'd like to use in the overall piece, the other accent beads that might be complimentary, and what kind of design statement you'd like to relay. You can envision whether a simple cord would look best, or if a more elaborate treatment would serve the design better. Trust me, because focal beads are so bold, they'll tell you all this information, so be sure to listen up.

Getting Started with Design

The inspiration for my designs always starts with my focal beads. Sometimes I can look at a bead and know immediately what to design, and other times I need to spend a little while with the bead until the design comes to me.

Often, the best place to start thinking about what you'll design is by starting with the color. The focal bead can dictate which hues to use. Typically you'll use similar or complementary colors, but other times a completely different colorway is best. (Is color a challenge for you? See the following pages to jumpstart your exploration.)

Next, think about what shape you want your piece to be. Should the focal bead sit along the strand horizontally, or maybe it would look best vertically? Would it serve the bead best to frame it with lots of strands, or would a simple strand look the nicest? Is the style of bead casual, elegant, subdued, or exuberant? The answer to those questions will definitely help you as you decide the shape of your piece.

Finally, decide on the length your creation will be. Sometimes it's best to find a piece you like and measure it to begin your design. Otherwise, a typical bracelet is about 8 inches (20.3 cm) long, and there are several different necklace lengths (choker = 16 inches [40.6 cm]; princess = 18 inches [45.7 cm]; matinee = 22 inches [55.9 cm]; opera = 30 inches [76.2 cm]; rope = 48 inches [121.9 cm]; and lariats are as long as you want them to be!). Keep in mind to include the length of your clasp in the final measurement if you're using one in your design.

Considering Color

When you use focal beads in your jewelry designs, you can often appreciate how easy it is to make color choices. After all, you're starting out with something quite striking to design around, and matching your accent beads to complement the colors of the focal bead is a no-brainer. Sometimes it's just that easy.

Still, some focal beads present a color challenge. I'll admit, I've been known to buy a bead (or two) on impulse, only to wonder later, what was I thinking? In these situations, I like to take the bead outside and look at it in the sunshine, or place it under a full-spectrum light. Many times a bead has hidden depths and colors I didn't notice when I bought it, so the creative challenge is on to design something fabulous.

For me, these challenging projects always begin with a brush-up in color theory. I start by deciding which color should be the dominant one in the piece. If the focal bead is totally blue, then the choice might be really easy. If it's half blue and half red, that might be easy, too, but I still consider making one color dominant. For example, blue with red accents might be even more attractive than going with all one color. Other times, I might be working with a bead that's a riot of different colors. I know I need to pick the ones to emphasize and the ones to play down, but which ones?

The best way to proceed is another color-theory standby: color temperature. Should the piece feature warm or cool colors? When I think of color temperature, I think of fire and ice: fire is warm (red, orange, and yellow) and ice is cool (blue, green, and some purples). This gives me a good sense of the feeling I want to bring out of the focal bead, and it helps me along in my color choice process. I do my best to avoid limiting myself to the 16 colors in a crayon box. Blue does not just mean navy, it also means turquoise, cornflower, and periwinkle. Green is not just pine green, but teal, lime, and glow-in-the-dark green. Red is not just crimson, but fuchsia, rose, and everything in between.

Once you've decided on the dominant color and temperature, take the next step into this little color theory lesson: color scheme. I have four favorite color schemes because 1) each is easy for me to remember, and 2) they are really hard to mess up! The schemes are called monochromatic, analogous, complementary, and triadic.

A monochromatic color scheme is the simplest scheme. You just use one color in the design. While this might sound boring at first, you can make a monochromatic design look very sophisticated by using different finishes, shapes, and sizes of beads.

Analogous is a similar color scheme, in my mind, to monochromatic. For this type you begin with one color and ooze over into the next two to four adjacent colors on a color wheel (figure 1). So, for example, with the monochromatic scheme, you would put blue beads around a blue focal bead. But with the analogous scheme, you might put green, blue-green, and yellow-green beads around a green focal bead.

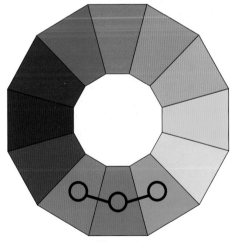

Figure 1

Complementary colors, as you may remember from school, are two opposite colors on a color wheel: blue and orange, purple and yellow, and red and green (figure 2). For a long time, I shied away from this color scheme; it reminded me too much of garish school football team uniforms. But then I realized that this scheme really does work well if you don't use the opposite colors in equal amounts. For example, a mostly green scheme with a splash of red can be terrific. The colors enhance each other without clashing.

The last color scheme I can always trust is the triadic (figure 3). These are a group of the primary colors (red, yellow, blue), the secondary colors (orange, green, and purple), or the tertiary colors (yellow green, red orange, blue violet, or the group of orange yellow, blue green, and red violet). The Mardi Gras Necklace on page 68 uses a triadic color scheme, because the bead itself has a triadic scheme, with blue the dominant color. That particular bead also has some green in it, which I chose to downplay in order to emphasize the triadic scheme.

Figure 2

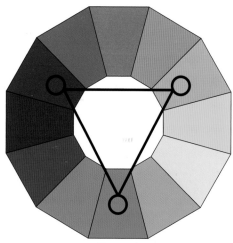

Figure 3

One more thing to consider when choosing a color scheme is the type of metal beads and findings you'll be including in your materials list. These components read as color, too. For instance, gold beads and findings really count as yellow, so they might not work with some color schemes. The same is true with all metals, since they usually take on some other color (copper can have an orange or brown cast, silver takes on blues, whites, and greens, etc.). For this reason never turn a blind eye to the effect metals can make on your overall color scheme.

So the next time you find yourself staring at a focal bead and wondering what to do with it, picture in your mind's eye what it would look like using each of these color schemes. To give yourself a creative charge, try not to rely on the same schemes too much, but challenge yourself by exploring one you've never used before.

Glass Focal Beads

Glass has fascinated people with its beauty since it was first produced over 4,500 years ago. As beaders, we're especially entranced! Today we continue to marvel at watery blown glass beads, hefty lampworked beads, and sparkling crystal beads.

There are as many types of glass focal beads as there are glassworkers, but there are four main types of glass focal beads found in most bead shops: blown glass, crystal, fused, and lampworked.

Blown Glass

Blown glass has held a special place in popular culture ever since its heyday in medieval Venice, with the enormous glass factories of Murano churning out stunning objects. The recent art glass movement has brought blown-glass bead makers to the forefront. Small-studio glass blowers usually begin the bead making process by heating their glass over a hot flame, then they add a bit of molten glass to the end of a glass blow pipe. Next, the beadmaker literally blows air into the tube to create a hollow form with the glass. The hot bead is shaped on each end to leave a hole for stringing. Despite their delicate look and light weight, most blown glass beads are very durable.

Crystal

The highest-quality crystal beads come from Austria. The best crystal glass has a 32% lead content, making light refract off the crystal in a quite dazzling way. Because lead makes glass softer, it's possible to cut crisp facets in the beads, adding even more to their sparkle. Crystal bead holes can be very sharp, so keep this in mind as you string a crystal focal bead—it can cut a single thread very easily.

Fused Glass

Fused-glass beads are created by layering cut or broken pieces of glass and melting them together in a glass kiln. The unique construction of this type of bead enables an artist to easily work with different glass colors and textures to create depth and richness. Fused glass beads can also be painted. The hole of a fused bead can be created by adding a ceramic fiber strip or bamboo skewer between layers before fusing or by drilling a hole after the bead has cooled. Fused beads must be annealed (the process of thoroughly heating, and then slowly cooling a piece of glass so it won't crack) just like blown and lampworked beads.

Lampworked Glass

Lampworked beads are created by using a hot torch to melt the end of a silicate- or borosilicate-based glass rod. The hot glass is then wound onto a thin piece of wire called a mandrel. Once cooled and annealed, the mandrel is removed, leaving a hole (otherwise it wouldn't be a bead).

Lampworking is one of the oldest ways to make glass beads, but it's taken on a wonderful resurgence in the last several years, especially in North America. Lampworkers have pushed the boundaries of the craft so that the variety, creativity, and availability of this type of glass bead are astounding.

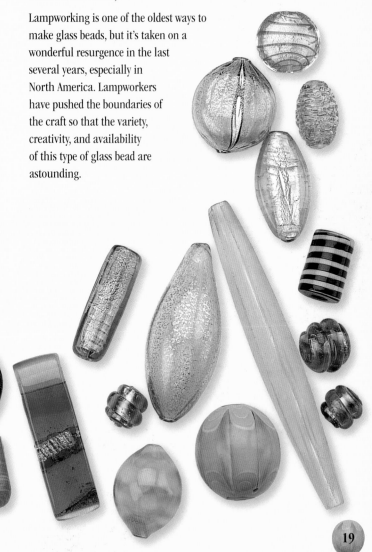

Glass focal beads shimmer, shine, and sparkle like no others. The focal beads shown here include all kinds of types, from the sophisticated Venetian foil-lined blown-glass ones (top left), to the more humble recycled glass one (bottom right).

Beading Techniques

There are just a few techniques you need to know that are essential to making the beautiful jewelry featured in *One Big Beautiful Bead*. Having these skills will ensure that your pieces are both strong and look professionally finished.

Wirework

Chances are you'll be working with wire when stringing beads, especially the large beads we're focusing on. Here are a few techniques you'll need to know in this book's projects.

Doris Coghill
Lea's Garden Necklace, 2002
12 x 6 x 1 inches (30.5 x 15.2 cm x 2.5 cm)
Seed beads, pressed glass beads, sterling beads;
Freeform multi-stringing with fringing
Photo by artist

Loops

Loops are created in order to connect a wire, head pin, or eye pin to something else, like another wire or a finding, as for bead dangles. They are also an integral part of the core strand technique (see page 23). Loops are created in all kinds of ways, but the following are the most common.

Simple Loops

1. Cut the wire so it exits ⅜ inch (9.0 mm) from the bead hole. Grasp the end of the wire with chain-nose pliers (or use your fingers) to make a 90° bend (see figure 4).

2. Use round-nose pliers to grasp the end of the wire. Turn your wrist completely over. The loop is complete once the wire tip touches the bend (see figure 5). *Note*: Always open a simple loop laterally, not horizontally, or you'll weaken the wire (see jump rings, figure 1, page 12).

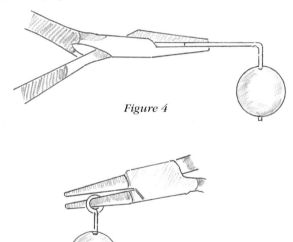

Figure 4

Figure 5

Wrapped Loops

1. Take the wire in one hand and chain-nose pliers in the other. Measure about ⅛ inch (3.0 mm) from the top of the last bead strung and bend the wire at a 90° angle (see figure 6). This ⅛ inch (3.0 mm) space is the loop's "neck."

2. Use round-nose pliers to grasp the wire at the bend you just made. Wrap the wire up and around the top jaw of the pliers (see figure 7). *Note:* Because the pliers' jaws are tapered, you can change the size of the loop by positioning the wire at different points on the pliers' jaws.

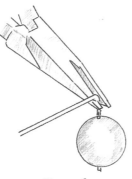

Figure 6

3. Hold the loop with the round-nose pliers and use your fingers or chain-nose pliers to tightly coil the tail wire around the neck so you make about three rotations (see figure 8).

4. Use the flush side of the wire cutters to trim the tail wire end close to the coil. Use chain-nose pliers to gently squeeze any excess wire into the coil so the exposed wire end won't scratch the wearer's skin or snag their clothing.

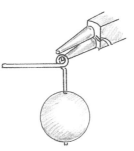

Figure 7

5. Use round- and chain-nose pliers to straighten and shape the loop until it looks the way you want it.

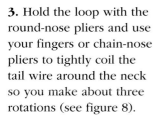

Figure 8

Crimping Wire

Crimping is one way to secure beading wire to a clasp or other finding. The technique utilizes a special type of bead called a crimp bead or crimp tube. It's possible to make the connection by simply squeezing crimp beads onto a wire using chain-nose pliers, but this makes a weak connection. Instead, use crimping pliers to do the job and you'll have strong results every time.

1. String one crimp bead and the finding onto flexible beading wire.

2. Pass the end of the wire back through the crimp bead in the opposite direction and move the bead down the wire so it sits about ⅛ inch (3.0 mm) from the finding. Leave a 1-inch (2.5 cm) tail of wire at the end.

3. Use crimping pliers to squeeze the bead with the U-shaped notch at the back of the pliers (see figure 9).

4. Turn the crimp bead so it's at a 90° angle to the pliers. Set it into the round notch at the front of the pliers. Squeeze the bead so it makes a nice, round tube (see figure 10).

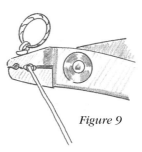

Figure 9

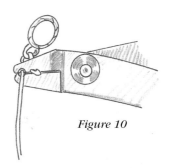

Figure 10

Ceramic Beads

People were making finely glazed ceramic beads 6,000 years ago. The Greeks were the first to coin the word: *keramikos* means pottery. Ceramic beads are made from clay (sometimes mixed with other materials), which are then usually glazed and fired in a kiln. If you're used to the uniformity of seed beads, ceramic beads can seem quite imperfect by comparison. You can use this as a design element; jewelry with ceramic beads can have a more organic, earthy, less machine-made feeling.

Faience

These beads, also known as mummy beads, were made by the ancient Egyptians and can still be found today. They are one of the simplest beads to make—a clay paste is dyed with earthy colors, shaped around reeds, and cut into sections. You have to be careful when using faience beads; they are not uniform in size (that's part of their charm), and tend to be a little fragile.

Raku

Because of their beautiful colors, raku beads are my all-time-favorite type of clay bead. Raku is made from clay, but unlike other types of ceramics, it is fired at a lower temperature, removed from the kiln while still glowing hot, and allowed to cool in the open air, or smoked by being poked into a bucket of sawdust, newspaper, or other flammable material. Raku beads are often molded into shapes such as faces or flowers. The process is as much at the mercy of nature as the artist, and no two pieces are ever exactly the same.

Porcelain

When I see a porcelain bead I often think of the blue-and-white porcelain tea set I had when I was a little girl. Just like that tea set, porcelain beads are made with very fine white or gray clay that has a silicate base. A liquid form of the clay, called slip, can be poured into a mold. It's dried, and then fired at an extremely high temperature to produce a bright white, very strong, translucent material that has many of the properties of glass. A porcelain bead artist often paints glazes onto the beads with a tiny paintbrush. The pieces are re-fired to take the glaze, and then are sometimes glazed and re-fired again.

Many porcelain beads are inexpensive, but there are some created by fine craftspeople that would qualify as true pieces of art. These porcelain beads are relatively expensive. You can find very beautiful hand-painted porcelain beads from China, often with a flower motif, and some are painted to resemble cloisonné, which is actually on an enamel design on metal.

Ceramic focal beads can bring an earthy feel to beaded works. That signature look can be achieved with organic, neutral-toned raku beads, hand-formed clay beads, as well as colorful Peruvian animal-shaped beads.

Core Strand

Many of the projects in this book start with what I like to call a "core strand." It's my favorite way to string beads because it provides an incredibly strong base.

1. Cut two pieces of metal wire each 3 inches (7.6 cm) long. Make a wrapped loop (see page 21) on one end of each wire. Set the two metal wires aside.

2. Determine the length you want the finished project to be. Add 6 inches (15.2 cm) to that figure, subtract the length of the clasp, and cut a piece of beading wire to that measurement.

3. String beads onto the beading wire as you desire. Finish with a bead that fits snugly into a cone. Leave an extra 3 inches (7.6 cm) of beading wire bare at each end of the piece. Place a clip at each end of the wire to keep the beads from falling off (see figure 11).

4. Remove the clip at one end of the beading wire. Use a surgeon's or figure-eight knot (see page 25) to tie the end to one of the wrapped loops. Pass the end of the beading wire back through the beads of the strand. Slide the beads to the knot you just made. Repeat the process for the other end of the beading wire (see figure 12).

5. String one cone on the straight end of one of the wrapped-loop wires. Snug the cone and start to make a wrapped loop. Before you finish the wrap, attach it to one end of the clasp or other finding (see figure 13). Finish the wrap so the cone is secured in place. Repeat at the other end of the piece.

6. If desired, embellish the strand using off-loom stitching techniques described on pages 25 to 28.

Figure 11

Figure 12

Figure 13

Tips

Save extra pieces of silver wire in a container or plastic bag—you can sell them back to some silver vendors. (Be sure not to mix up your sterling and fine silver!)

Off-Loom Beadwork

Sometimes you just can't do a focal bead justice by simply stringing it. If you want to make a statement, off-loom beadwork is a great way to go. You don't use a bead loom to create this kind of beadwork. You just use a needle, thread, and some stitches to weave beads (usually seed beads) together into flat pieces, tubes, spirals, fringe … you name it. Off-loom bead-work, or "beadweaving," is a lot of fun, and even though it's fairly easy to do, people will never believe it. Just let them keep thinking you're a genius. Truly, once you learn one stitch and see how easy it is, you'll want to learn others. The stitches covered in this book are among the easiest and most instantly gratifying.

General Beadweaving Know-How

Anyone who works with beads, a needle, and thread needs to have several general skills in her repertoire.

Going in the Right Direction

When the instructions say "pass the needle through," the needle and thread should go through the bead in the same direction as it was strung. If the instructions say "pass the needle back through," the needle and thread should go through the bead in the opposite direction.

Tying Off Old Threads

When making a multiple-strand piece or one that incorporates beadweaving, you'll probably run out of thread before you finish. Try to keep the threads well-hidden within the beads so you can't tell where the threads end or begin.

1. While your thread is still longer than the length of your beading needle, pass the needle underneath the existing thread between two beads, creating a loop. Pass the needle through the loop and draw it tight to make an overhand knot (see page 25). Pass the needle through the next bead and gently tug the thread to hide the knot inside the bead (see figure 14). Pass the needle through several adjacent beads. If you have enough thread and you want to make sure your thread is extra secure, you can make additional knots in the same manner.

2. Pull the thread tight and use scissors to trim the thread close to the work so the thread end disappears inside the bead. *Note*: The best place to tie off is next to a large bead, like a size 6° or accent bead.

Beginning a New Thread

1. Cut a comfortable working length of thread and pass it through the beading needle. If you like working with doubled thread, pair the ends. Tie a knot in the end of the thread and cut off the tail(s) close to the knot. If desired, place a tiny bit of clear nail polish on the knot to seal it.

2. Pass the needle through a bead near the place you'd like to resume your stitching, preferably next to a large bead. Pass the needle underneath the existing thread between two beads, creating a loop. Pass the needle through the loop and draw it tight to make an overhand knot (see page 25).

3. Pass the needle through the adjacent bead and gently tug the thread to hide the knot inside the bead. Pass the needle through several adjacent beads until you can exit from your new starting point.

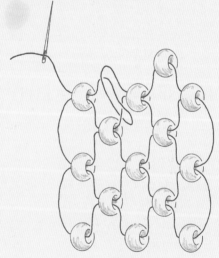

Figure 14

Knots

You'll need to know how to make several different knots to complete the projects in this book.

Figure-eight knots are created by crossing the thread ends to make a small loop. Wrap the thread that lies on top around the bottom one. Pass the thread through the initial loop from the top (see figure 15). Pull it tight.

Figure 15

Overhand knots are made by forming a loop with the thread and then passing the thread ends through the loop (see figure 16). Pull it tight.

Figure 16

Square knots start with an overhand knot, with the right end over the left end. Make another overhand knot, this time with the left end over the right end (see figure 17). Pull it tight.

Figure 17

Surgeon's knots are actually very strong square knots. First make an overhand knot, with the right end over the left end, but wrap the thread around itself several times. Finish the knot as you would a square knot, with the left end over the right end (see figure 18). Pull it tight.

Figure 18

Off-Loom Stitches

Fringe, peyote stitch, and different spirals are great ways to bring out the beauty of your focal bead. Once you feel comfortable with a few different stitches, experiment with adding them together—you'll find it a great way to express your own unique creativity.

Fringe

Fringe is a common embellishment for off-loom beading. There are a myriad of different types. Here is the most common.

1. Exit the needle and thread from the point on the beadwork where you'd like to add the fringe. String on your desired length of beads.

2. Skip the last bead strung and pass the needle back through the rest of the beads you just strung.

3. Pass the needle back into the beadworked base, close to where you last exited (see figure 19).

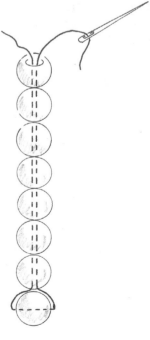

Figure 19

Peyote Stitch

Peyote stitch is one of the easiest and most versatile stitches ever! It comes in several varieties, two of which are flat. One works with an even count of beads and the other an odd count.

I find that the easiest way to learn peyote stitch is by using black and white size 5° cube beads. Follow the instructions below, and you'll get the hang of the stitch in no time

Flat Even-Count Peyote Stitch

1. Thread 2 feet (61.0 cm) of thread in a beading needle and double it. Place a clip 3 inches (7.6 cm) from the end of the thread.

2. String on one black bead and one white bead. Repeat five more times. These beads make up the first two rows.

3. String on one white bead and pass the needle back through the last black bead you strung in step 2 (see figure 20).

4. String on one white bead and pass the needle through the next black bead from step 2. Repeat to the end of the row. When you reach the end of the row, string on one black bead and pass the needle through the last white bead you added in the previous row (see figure 21).

5. Repeat steps 3 and 4 to continue adding rows.

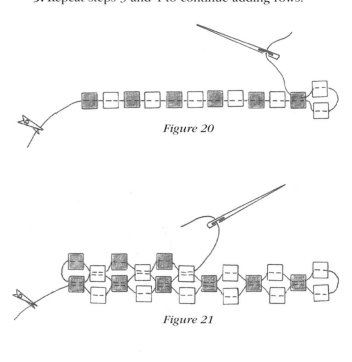

Figure 20

Figure 21

Flat Odd-Count Peyote Stitch

1. Thread 2 feet (61.0 cm) of thread in a beading needle and double it. Place a clip 3 inches (7.6 cm) from the end of the thread.

2. String on one black bead and one white bead. Repeat five more times. String on one black bead. These beads make up the first two rows.

3. String on one black bead and pass the needle back through the last white bead you strung in step 2.

4. String on one black bead and pass the needle through the next white bead from step 2. Repeat to the end of the row. When you reach the end of the row, pass the needle through the last bead of the row below. Weave through the beads and pass the needle back through the bead you just added so you can work the next row.

5. Work the fourth row across as usual, make the turnaround, and start the fifth row. When you come to the end of the fifth row, string on the last bead. To set up for the next row you can either weave through the beads as you did in step 4, or simply pass the needle under the thread that connects the previous two rows. Pass the needle back through the bead you just added and work across as usual (see figure 22).

Freeform Peyote Stitch

Once you've created a beaded base by stitching a few peyote-stitched rows, you can take your beading to an even more creative level by working in a freeform manner. You can accomplish this in all kinds of ways. One way is to embellish the base by exiting from a base bead, stringing on several beads, and passing through the base at another point. You can make fringe off the base. And you can use differently sized beads on the same row to give the beadwork a textured or ruffled look.

Experiment with colors. Try whatever you think looks good. Anything goes, because with this technique, you really can't make a mistake. It takes on its own personality, and your freeform piece will never look like anyone else's (see figure 23).

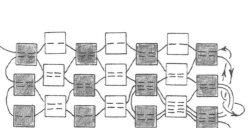

Figure 22

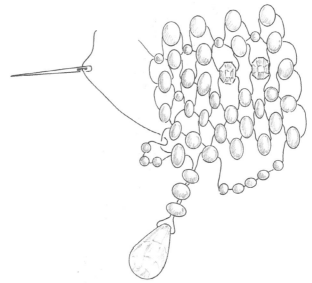

Figure 23

Spiral Ropes

Spiral ropes, in all their variety, never cease to amaze me with their simple elegance. They look great paired with many types of focal beads. Couple a beautiful focal bead with a spiral rope, and an endless array of design possibilities might open up before you.

Simple Spiral Rope

This spiraling cord is sometimes called "Internet Stitch" from its online popularity years ago. It's easy to learn and works up much faster than most spiral ropes.

One beauty of this spiral is that you can easily change its look by varying the color, size, and types of beads you use. It's a wonderful way to embellish a piece that's been made with the core strand technique described on page 23.

1. Use thread and a beading needle or flexible beading wire to string on enough size 6° beads to serve as your core strand. Tie each end to a wrapped loop as in the Core Strand technique and set aside.

2. Thread a beading needle with a 2-foot (61.0 cm) length of single or double thread. Tie a knot in the end.

3. Secure the end of the thread onto the wrapped loop at one end of the core strand. Pass the needle through four beads so you exit between the fourth and fifth beads of the core strand.

4. String on three size 11° beads, one accent bead, and three size 11° beads. Pass the needle down through the second bead on the core strand and continue down through three more core strand beads so you exit between the fifth and sixth core strand beads.

5. Repeat step 4, stringing on seven beads, passing the needle through the next bead down on the core strand and down through three more beads (see figure 24). Repeat to add loops all the way down the core strand. Always push your loops to one side to create the spiral effect.

6. Once you near the end of the core strand, end the spiral by simply tying off the thread.

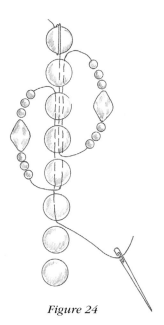

Figure 24

To Spiral, or Not to Spiral?

You can go for the traditional spiral look—or not. If you like the spiral, simply be sure to push all your loops in the same direction as you work, and you'll get results. If you're not too concerned about getting a perfect spiral, it will look fabulous anyway: On my very first simple spiral stitch necklace, I didn't realize until about a third of the way down that you had to keep pushing the loop one way to get the spiral. Nobody but me ever noticed that the beads went every which way!

Plastic Focal Beads

I don't usually recommend using plastic beads in your designs, especially the dime-a-dozen kind you find at the local hobby shop. That said, there are gorgeous vintage plastic and modern resin beads available on the market, and of course, my favorite—handmade polymer clay beads.

Vintage

Bakelite was one of the first plastics created in the early 1900s. It was mostly used in industry, but by the 1930s made its way to the jewelry world, too. It comes in amber to brown colors and is now highly collectible. You can tell if it's true Bakelite if you smell formaldehyde when you dip it in hot water.

Acrylic beads, also known as Lucite and Plexiglass, are another type of high-quality plastic bead. Acrylics were fashionable during the 1960s and are very common as vintage non-glass focal beads. Acrylic starts as a transparent plastic, but is easily dyed and molded, so comes in a wide variety of transparent and opaque colors and thousands of shapes.

Some of the finest vintage plastic beads come from Japan and Germany. Look for beads with little or no seam, smooth edges, and color that has been added to (not painted on) the bead itself.

Polymer Clay

Polymer clay works up like regular silicate clay, but is made from polyvinyl chloride (PVC) and comes in dozens of pre-dyed colors. It's fired at such a low temperature that a well-ventilated studio and a toaster oven is all that's required to get started. Polymer clay has outgrown its simple beginnings in craft shops, and has blossomed into the art realm. In the right hands, polymer clay can imitate stone, lampworked or fused glass, raku, and all

other types of beads. This type of focal bead is very lightweight, so it is practical to string on thread alone, unlike heavier beads.

Resin

Like acrylic, resin beads are technically plastic, but in recent times the term "resin beads" refers to a specific type of colorful, translucent, frosted-looking bead that comes in a wide variety of shapes. As focal beads, they are very lightweight, so they don't require super-strong stringing techniques. These beads are nontoxic and aren't prone to breakage.

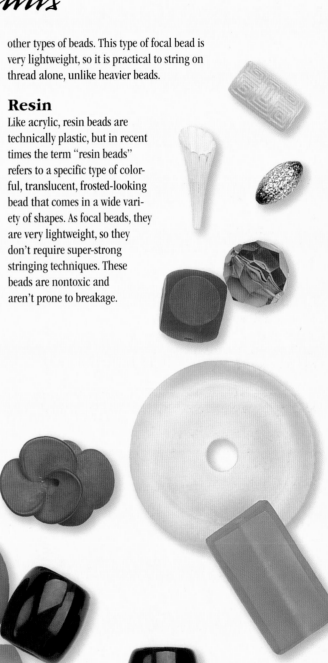

Using a plastic focal bead is a great way to keep a piece from becoming overly heavy. The choices are many, from great-looking retro (top right) and modern (donut and cube at middle right) resin beads, to popular handmade polymer clay beads (see projects on pages 37 and 46).

Russian Spiral Rope

The Russian Spiral is another very quick and easy way to make a beaded rope. It works with any size bead, but I've found that size 11° and size 8° beads work best. For this sample, use black size 11° beads and white size 8° beads.

1. Thread a beading needle with 3 feet (.9 m) of doubled thread.

2. String on one black bead, one white bead, two black beads, one white bead, two black beads, one white bead, and one black bead for a total of nine beads in all. Tie the ends into a knot to make a tight foundation circle. Pass the needle through the first bead you strung in this step.

3. String on one white bead and two black beads. Pass the needle through the next black bead of the foundation circle. String on one white bead and two black beads. Pass the needle through the first black bead from the next three-bead set of the foundation circle. Continue around and finish by exiting from the first bead you exited in this step. You have completed round 2.

4. To start round 3, string on one white bead and two black beads. Pass the needle through the first black bead added in round 2. String on one white bead and two black beads and pass the needle through the first black bead of the second set of three beads you added in the previous round. Repeat around (see figure 25).

5. Repeat step 4 to create as long a rope as desired. When you've reached the end, weave through the beads from the last round to make a tight circle at the end of the tube. Weave back through beads on the rope and tie it off.

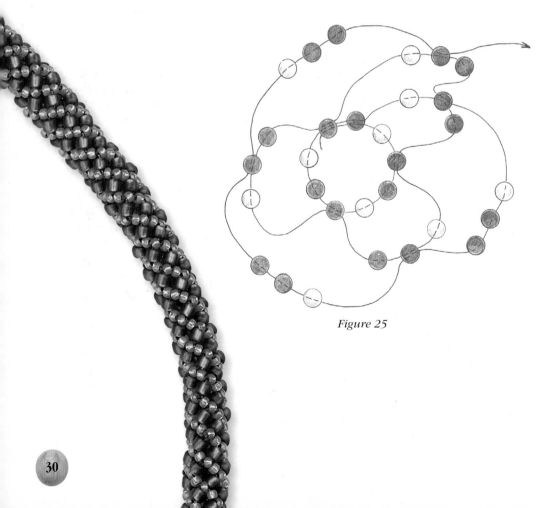

Figure 25

30

Metal Focal Beads

Silver beads, gold beads, brass beads—metal beads are great on their own, and great with every other type of bead you can think of. Since you'll probably often use metal findings in your jewelry, adding some matching metal accent beads will make your design more harmonious. Or you can make a bold statement by featuring a large metal focal bead.

Base Metal

There are noble metals (gold and silver) and there are base metals. The noble metals are expensive and do not corrode. The base metals are relatively inexpensive and will oxidize or corrode. You want to be careful about using base metals in your jewelry, as some people are allergic to them. Base metals include copper, brass, and pewter. Copper is generally considered a base metal because it oxidizes (turns green) easily. Copper focal beads, however, can be very striking, especially when combined with other types of beads.

Brass (an alloy of zinc and copper) has two advantages over other metal beads: it's inexpensive and has a color similar to real gold. Brass beads often come from Africa and India. Even though brass is generally cheap, certain types of African brass focal beads are highly collectible and therefore correspondingly expensive.

Pewter is mostly tin, with some copper and other metals added in. It can look like silver, but it is much softer. The cheapest types of pewter have lead additives, so keep that in mind when you buy and use pewter focal beads – you especially would not want to leave them anywhere a small child might swallow them (good advice for all beads, really).

Gold

Gold by itself is very soft, so typically it is combined with another metal to make it stronger. Gold beads come in gold-plated, gold vermeil, and gold-filled. Gold-plated is brass or copper covered with a very thin layer of gold. You have to be careful where you use gold-plated beads; the gold will wear off if it's placed anywhere where it is likely to be rubbed often. Vermeil is similar to gold-plated, except the metal underneath the thin layer is silver. Gold-filled beads are really the opposite of what they sound like. The beads aren't filled with gold, but have a base metal core with a layer of gold on the outside that's been heat and pressure-applied. This type of focal bead has a much thicker layer of gold than gold-plated beads and will stand up better to daily wear and tear.

Metal Art Clay

Metal art clay is a fairly new invention: it's composed of fine silver or gold powder mixed with an organic binder to make clay. This clay can be molded into very interesting designs that would be difficult, if not impossible, in sheet-metal form. The clay is dried and baked in a kiln, where the binder burns away and leaves fine silver. This type of silver is very porous, and you can buy beads with perfume added. Metal clay focal beads have the same properties as fine silver beads.

Silver

Silver, I must admit, is my favorite metal. More affordable and versatile than gold, I find its icy beauty goes with every type of bead. Silver comes in fine, sterling, and silver-plated. Silver-plated is exactly like gold-plated, in that a brass or copper core is covered with a layer of silver.

People often think that sterling silver is the most valuable; in fact, it is silver with copper added (92.5 percent silver and 7.5 percent copper, to be exact) to make it stronger. Fine silver is pure silver, and you will often see fine silver marked with a ".999" stamp to indicate that it is fine silver, not sterling. The Karen Hill Tribe in Thailand makes amazing fine silver, or "Thai silver" beads, in a wide variety of shapes including flowers and animals. They are often referred to as "Hill Tribe silver" also.

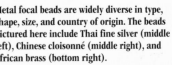

Metal focal beads are widely diverse in type, shape, size, and country of origin. The beads pictured here include Thai fine silver (middle left), Chinese cloisonné (middle right), and African brass (bottom right).

Dutch Spiral Rope

Dutch spiral is a very pretty, very open spiral. Its name is inspired by the woman in the Netherlands who popularized the stitch several years ago, but it's also known as Cellini Spiral or Twisted Chain Peyote Stitch. You can use any combination of seed and other small beads for this technique to vary the look. For this sample, I've used size 5° cube beads, size 5° hex beads, size 6° round seed beads, size 8° hex beads, size 11° seed beads, and size 15° seed beads.

1. Organize your beads into little piles by size, largest to smallest.

2. Thread a beading needle with 3 feet (.9 m) of doubled thread. String on one size 5° cube bead, one size 5° hex bead, one size 6° seed bead, one size 8° hex bead, one size 11° seed bead, one size 15° seed bead, one size 11° seed bead, and one size 5° cube bead. Tie a knot to form a tight foundation circle, leaving a 6-inch (15.2 cm) tail. Pass the needle through the first bead you strung in this step.

3. String on one size 5° hex bead and pass the needle through the size 5° hex bead from the foundation circle. String on one size 6° seed bead and pass the needle through the size 6° seed bead from the foundation circle. String on one size 5° hex bead and pass the needle through the size 5° hex bead from the foundation circle.

4. String on one size 11° seed bead, one size 15° seed bead, one size 11° seed bead, and one size 5° cube bead. Pass the needle through the first cube bead you added in this round (see figure 26). This small strand will make up all of your increases and decreases.

5. Repeat steps 3 and 4 to make two more rounds. *Note*: You won't always end your rounds by exiting from a size 5° cube bead as you did in step 4. Instead, because you're beading a spiral, you'll just continue spiraling into the next rounds by stringing on the same type of bead you're about to stitch into, much like climbing a spiral staircase. It will help you keep your place if you remember that you'll always make an increase or decrease in that same stranded section as noted in step 4.

6. Repeat steps 3 and 4 for two more rounds, but this time string on two size 11° seed beads, one size 15° seed bead, two size 11° seed beads, and one size 5° cube bead in the increase/decrease section (as noted in step 4). See figure 27.

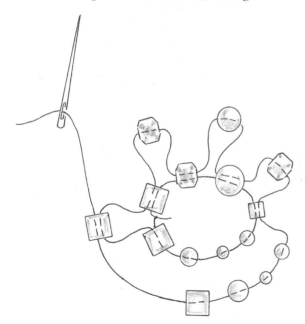

Figure 26

Figure 27

7. Repeat steps 3 and 4 for three rounds, this time stringing on three size 11° seed beads, one size 15° seed bead, three size 11° seed beads, and one size 5° cube bead in the increase/decrease section.

8. Repeat steps 3 and 4 for three rounds, this time stringing on four size 11° seed beads, one size 15° seed bead, four size 11° seed beads, and one size 5° cube bead in the increase/decrease section.

9. Repeat steps 3 and 4 for as many rounds as desired, always stringing on five size 11° seed beads, one size 15° seed bead, five size 11° seed beads, and one size 5° cube bead in the increase/decrease section.

10. Repeat steps 5 to 8 in reverse to make the rope's width decrease. Weave through the beads and tie off the thread.

Diving In

Now that you've got all the technical know-how you need to make the projects in *One Big Beautiful Bead*, you're ready to dive in and start creating. Because each focal bead is a unique find, you may not be able to exactly duplicate the projects in the book. But you could try starting off by first choosing your favorite project, inserting your own focal bead into the mix, and then copying the rest of the jewelry design as shown. Or let these gorgeous projects inspire you to design your own unique piece.

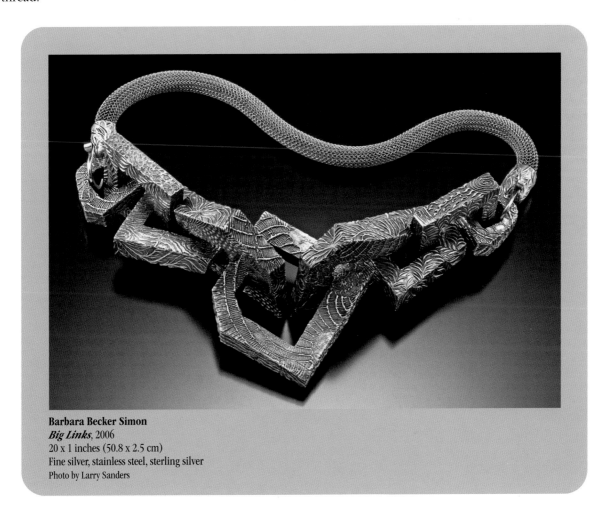

Barbara Becker Simon
Big Links, 2006
20 x 1 inches (50.8 x 2.5 cm)
Fine silver, stainless steel, sterling silver
Photo by Larry Sanders

Lapis Queen

This jumble of lapis lazuli and freshwater pearl beads, paired with a weighty silver slider and coordinating silver drum beads, makes an impressive statement, but the technique is very straightforward and easy to do. The result? A necklace fit for a queen that's easy enough to make in an evening.

Materials

1 Hill Tribe fine silver 35 mm x 63 mm slider bead with a floral design

2 sterling silver 14 mm x 16 mm drum beads with dragonfly and shell designs

28 lapis lazuli 8 mm round beads

4 lapis lazuli 8 mm saucer beads

48 navy 7 mm freshwater pearl round beads

95 lapis lazuli 4 mm round beads

30 sterling silver 4 mm melon beads

60 sterling silver 2 mm seamless round beads

1 tube of clear silver-lined size 11° seed beads

2 sterling silver 10 mm x 18 mm cones with a floral design

1 sterling silver inch 25 mm S clasp

54 inches (1.4 m) of .014-inch (.036 cm) flexible beading wire

6 inches (15.2 cm) of 20-gauge sterling silver wire

1 spool of dark blue beading thread

Tools

Wire cutters

Chain-nose pliers

Round-nose pliers

2 bead clips

Scissors

Size 10 beading needle

Finished Length

20½ inches (52.1 cm)

Preparing the Components

1 Use the wire cutters to cut the flexible beading wire into two 27-inch (68.6 cm) lengths. Set them aside.

2 Use the wire cutters to cut the sterling silver wire into two 3-inch (7.6 cm) pieces. Use the chain- and round-nose pliers to form a wrapped loop (see page 21) on one end of each wire. Set them aside.

Stringing the First Strand

3 Place a clip on one of the beading wire lengths 3 inches (7.6 cm) from one end. String on one round 8 mm lapis bead. String on a sequence of one seed bead and one 4 mm lapis bead. Repeat this sequence 26 more times, and then string on one seed bead, one lapis saucer, one drum bead, and one lapis saucer.

4 String on a sequence of one seed bead and one 4 mm lapis bead. Repeat this sequence twenty more times, and then string on one seed bead. String on the slider bead so it covers the beads you just strung.

5 Repeat step 3 in reverse.

6 Check the design and make any adjustments. Make sure there is an equal amount of bare beading wire on each end. Place a clip at each end of the wire.

Lapis Queen

7 Remove one of the clips and use a figure-eight knot (see page 25) to tie the wire end to one of the wrapped loops. Remove the other clip. Snug the beads and use a figure-eight knot to tie the open wire end to the second wrapped loop. Set the strand aside.

Stringing the Second Strand

8 Cut a 3-foot (.9 m) length of the thread and pass it through the needle. Double the thread and tie a knot in the end. Tie the end of the thread to one of the wrapped loops at the end of the first strand. Pass the needle through the 8 mm lapis bead at the end of the strand.

9 String on a sequence of one 2 mm round bead and one pearl bead. Repeat this sequence eighteen more times, and then string on one 2 mm round bead. Pass the needle through the first lapis saucer, the drum bead, and the second lapis saucer on the first strand.

10 String on a sequence of one 2 mm round bead and one pearl bead. Repeat this sequence four more times, and then string on one 2 mm bead.

11 String on a sequence of one seed bead and one 4 mm lapis bead. Repeat this sequence nine more times. String on a sequence of one 2 mm round bead and one pearl bead. Repeat this sequence four more times, and then string on one 2 mm bead. Pass the needle through the slider bead.

12 Pass the needle through the third lapis spacer, the second drum bead, and the fourth lapis spacer of the first strand.

13 Repeat step 9. Pass the needle through the round 8 mm lapis bead at the end of the first strand and securely tie the thread onto the second wrapped loop.

Stringing the Third Strand

14 Use a figure-eight knot to tie the end of the second length of beading wire to one of the wrapped loops. Pass the wire through the round 8 mm lapis bead at the end of the strand.

15 String on one 2 mm bead. String on a sequence of one melon bead and one round 8 mm lapis bead. Repeat this sequence ten more times. String on one melon bead and one 2 mm bead. Pass the wire through the first lapis spacer, the drum bead, and the second lapis spacer on the first strand.

16 String on one 2 mm bead, one melon bead, one round 8 mm lapis bead, one melon bead, one round 8 mm lapis bead, one melon bead, and one 2 mm bead.

17 String on a sequence of one seed bead and one 4 mm lapis bead. Repeat this sequence nine more times.

18 Repeat step 16 in reverse. Pass the wire through the slider bead.

19 Repeat steps 14 and 15 in reverse, passing through the third lapis spacer, the second drum bead, and the fourth lapis spacer on the first strand.

Completing the Core Strand

20 Weave any tail threads or wires back into the strands and trim any excess.

21 String on one cone, from inside to outside, on one of the wrapped loop wires.

22 Tighten the cone against the beadwork and use the chain- and round-nose pliers to make a wrapped loop that attaches to one half of the S clasp (see Making a Core Strand, page 23).

23 Repeat steps 21 and 22 to complete the other side of the necklace.

Mandala Mix Necklace

This necklace features freeform peyote stitch. The stitching creates a kaleidoscope of colors and textures that resonates with the focal bead's kaleidoscopic imagery. The polymer clay focal bead is so light that beading thread is sufficient. Making multiple passes through the focal bead also helps support it.

Stringing the Base

1 Cut a 3-foot (.9 m) length of the beading thread, pass it through the needle, and double it. Place a clip 6 inches (15.2 cm) from the end of the thread.

2 String on a mixture of seed beads in various sizes and colors for 2¾ inches (7.0 cm). This mixture of beads is the base from which you'll work freeform peyote stitch (see page 27). It's best to keep to an odd number of beads here.

3 String on 1 inch (2.5 cm) of size 11° seed beads in one color to make the first strand segment.

4 String on ½ inch (1.3 cm) of topaz size 6° seed beads, one polymer bicone bead, and ½ inch (1.3 cm) of orange size 6° seed beads.

5 String on ½ inch (1.3 cm) of size 11° seed beads in one color to make the second strand segment.

6 String on a mixture of seed beads in various sizes and col-

Materials

1 purple, red, orange, and white 43 mm polymer clay flat polygon focal bead

2 purple, white, and gold 12 mm x 26 mm polymer clay long bicone beads

2 purple, red, white, and gold 10 mm x 13 mm polymer clay bicone beads

2 orange 4 mm faceted fire-polished beads

1 tube of transparent orange size 5° cube beads 1 tube of purple AB size 5° triangle beads

1 tube of frosted orange size 6° seed beads

1 tube of topaz AB size 6° seed beads

1 tube of purple AB size 8° triangle seed beads

1 tube of purple silver-lined size 11° seed beads

1 tube of transparent orange size 11° seed beads

1 silver 15 mm shank button with a floral design

1 spool of beading thread to match the beads

Tools

Scissors

Size 10 beading needle

Finished Length

21 inches (53.0 cm)

ors for 2 inches (5.1 cm). String on one long bicone bead.

7 String on a sequence of 13 purple size 11° seed beads and five orange size 11° seed beads twice in a row. Then string on 13 purple size 11° seed beads. This is the third and longest strand segment, where you will attach the focal bead.

8 Repeat steps 2 to 7 in reverse to string the other side of the necklace.

Embellishing the Base

9 Work freeform peyote stitch down the base strand until you reach your first strand segment. String a strand of size 11° seed beads of equal length, and continue working freeform peyote stitch down the base.

10 When you reach a polymer clay bead, pass the needle through it. Continue working freeform peyote stitch and stringing strands of equal length when you reach the strand segments. Repeat down the necklace.

11 Work up and down the necklace for at least five passes. Note: I found that the holes in my small polymer clay beads would only allow me to pass through four times. On the fifth pass, I strung a strand of size 11° seed beads and, skipping the polymer clay bead completely, started in on the next section of peyote stitch. Embellishing the peyote-stitched sections with strands helps to carry the look throughout.

Adding the Button/Loop Clasp

12 Once you're satisfied with the design, start a new thread at one end of the necklace and exit from one of the end beads. String on six purple size 11° seed beads, the button, and six more purple size 11° seed beads. Pass the needle back into an end bead on the peyote-stitched portion, and out from the first bead you exited in this step. Weave through all the beads you just added one or two more times to reinforce it. Tie off the thread (see figure 1).

13 Start a new thread at the other end of the necklace and exit from one of the end beads. String on enough purple size 11° seed beads to make a loop wide enough to snugly pass over the button. Pass the needle back into an end bead on the peyote-stitched portion, and out from the first bead you exited in this step. Weave through all the beads you just added one or two more times to reinforce it. Tie off the thread (see figure 2).

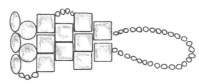

Figure 1

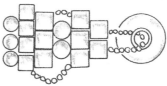

Figure 2

Making the Center Dangle

14 Cut a 1-foot (30.5 cm) length of thread, pass it through the needle, and double it. Place a clip 4 inches (10.2 cm) from the end of the thread.

15 String on one fire-polished bead, the focal bead, one fire-polished bead, and ten size 5° triangle seed beads. Make a loop by passing back through the second fire-polished bead you just strung and the focal bead. Before tightening, slip the loop over the longest strand segment at the center of the necklace. Tie two square knots (see page 000). Pass the needle through the first fire-polished bead you strung. String on one purple size 11° seed bead. Pass the needle up through the rest of the beads and tie it off (see figure 3). Thread the tail end on the needle, weave through the beads a few times to reinforce it, and tie it off.

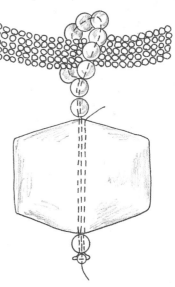

Figure 3

High Tea Necklace

You may feel like you're attending a garden tea party every time you wear this piece. The necklace showcases a lovely set of delicate floral beads up front, accented by strands of shining, faceted crystals to support the design.

Materials

1 lavender 10 mm x 18 mm lampworked glass focal bead with dots

2 pink and green 8 mm x 14 mm lamp-worked glass focal beads with floral designs

2 lavender 7 mm x 15 mm lampworked glass focal beads with dots

2 gold-filled 9 mm Bali-style bead caps (or sized to fit the focal bead)

2 gold-filled 10 mm Bali-style daisy spacers

2 gold-filled 3 mm x 8 mm Bali-style rondelles

60 lavender 4 mm x 7 mm crystal rondelles

1 tube of transparent lavender size 11° seed beads

2 gold-filled 9 mm x 16 mm cones with filigree

1 gold-filled 34 mm S clasp

24 inches (61.0 cm) of .014-inch (.036 cm) flexible beading wire

6 inches (15.2 cm) of 20-gauge gold-filled wire

Tools

Wire cutters

Chain-nose pliers

Round-nose pliers

2 bead clips

Finished Length

18 inches (45.7 cm)

Preparing the Components

1 Use the wire cutters to cut the gold-filled wire into two 3-inch (7.6 cm) pieces.

2 Use the chain- and round-nose pliers to form a wrapped loop (see page 21) at one end of each wire. Set them aside.

Stringing the Beads

3 Place a clip 3 inches (7.6 cm) from one end of the flexible beading wire. String on a sequence of one crystal rondelle and one seed bead. Repeat the sequence 27 more times. Then string on one gold rondelle, one 7 mm x 15 mm lampworked bead, one 10 mm spacer, and one 8 mm x 14 mm lampworked bead.

4 String on one bead cap from the outside in, the focal bead, and one bead cap from the inside out.

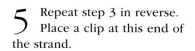

5 Repeat step 3 in reverse. Place a clip at this end of the strand.

6 Check the design and make any adjustments. Make sure there is an equal amount of bare beading wire on each side of the strand.

Completing the Core Strand

7 Remove the clip from one end of the strand. Use a figure-eight knot (see page 25) to tightly tie one end of the beading wire to one of the wrapped loops. Snug the beads and repeat to attach the other end of the necklace to the second wrapped loop. If possible, pass the beading wire back through the beads on the strand. Trim any excess beading wire.

8 String on one cone, from in-side to outside, on one of the wrapped loop wires.

9 Tighten the cone against the beadwork and use the chain-and round-nose pliers to make a wrapped loop that attaches to one half of the S clasp (see Making a Core Strand, page 23).

10 Repeat steps 8 and 9 to complete the other side of the necklace.

Verdant Spirals Necklace

Stitch an elegant Dutch spiral rope to complement a spiral motif focal bead. Constructing this necklace is very straightforward, and being able to wear it is worth every stitch.

Making the Spiral Rope

1 Organize your seed beads by size, from largest to smallest.

2 Working with your beads from smallest to largest, use the needle and thread to stitch two 8-inch (20.3 cm) lengths of Dutch spiral rope as described on page 31. Set the ropes aside.

Stringing the Necklace

3 Use the flexible beading wire to string on the focal bead and slide it to the center of the wire.

4 String on one bead cap from outside to inside on one end of the beading wire. Repeat for the other side of the focal bead. (The caps should cup away from the focal bead.) Place a clip next to one of the bead caps.

Materials

1 green glass focal bead, 24 mm x 47 mm long

1 tube of frosted peridot size 5° cube beads

1 tube of transparent clear size 5° hex beads 1 tube of luster peridot size 6° seed beads

1 tube of transparent dark green size 8° hex beads 1 tube of transparent peridot size 8° seed beads

1 tube of frosted silver-lined size 11° seed beads

1 tube of frosted peridot size 15° cylinder beads

2 sterling silver 7 mm x 14 mm bead caps (or to fit the focal bead)

2 sterling silver 14 mm x 14 mm cones with a twisted wire pattern

1 sterling silver 25 mm S clasp

1 small spool of beading thread to match the beads

28 inches (71.0 cm) of .010-inch (.025 cm) flexible beading wire

6 inches (15.2 cm) of 20-gauge sterling silver wire

Tools

Size 10 or 12 beading needle

Scissors

2 bead clips

Wire cutters

Chain-nose pliers

Round-nose pliers

Finished Length

21¼ inches (54.0 cm)

Verdant Spirals Necklace

5 Pass the unclipped beading wire end through three adjacent beads (the two cube beads and one size 6° seed bead work well) of the foundation circle at one end of one of the spiral ropes.

6 Pass the beading wire up the middle of the tube and string on enough size 8° seed beads to reach the length of the rope. (These beads constitute the core strand.)

7 Repeat step 5 to attach the beading wire to the other end of the spiral rope and place a clip at the end of the wire. Weaving through the spiral rope beads ensures that the rope doesn't collapse on itself vertically.

8 Remove the clip at the other side of the focal bead. Repeat steps 5 to 7 to attach the other spiral rope to the other side of the focal bead. Set the assembly aside.

Completing the Core Strand

9 Use the wire cutters to cut the sterling silver wire into two 3-inch (7.6 cm) pieces. Use the chain- and round-nose pliers to form a wrapped loop (see page 21) at one end of each wire.

10 Use a figure-eight knot (see page 25) to tightly tie one end of the beading wire to one of the wrapped loops. Snug the beads and repeat to attach the other end of the necklace to the second wrapped loop. If possible, pass the beading wire back through the beads on the core strand. Trim any excess beading wire.

11 String on one cone, from inside to outside, on one of the wrapped loop wires.

12 Tighten the cone against the beadwork and use the chain- and round-nose pliers to make a wrapped loop that attaches to one half of the S clasp (see Making a Core Strand, page 23).

13 Repeat steps 11 and 12 to complete the other side of the necklace.

Tightrope Walker Necklace

Sometimes a focal bead is so special that framing it with too many other beads would only detract from its beauty. In this case, an artfully-sculpted polymer clay face bead need only hang from a simple leather cord to make a balanced, yet striking look.

Materials

1 silver, white, and burgundy 12 mm x 22 mm polymer clay focal bead

1 crimson 4 mm fire-polished bead

1 sterling silver 4 mm x 8 mm patterned saucer bead

1 sterling silver 4 mm Bali-style daisy spacer

1 sterling silver 8 mm filigree bead cap

1 sterling silver 3-inch (7.6 cm) 22-gauge head pin with a ball tip

1 black 16-inch (40.6 cm) 4 mm round leather cord with a sterling silver clasp

Tools

Chain-nose pliers

Round-nose pliers

Wire cutters

Finished Length

16 inches (40.6 cm)

Making the Dangle

1 Use the head pin to string the daisy spacer, the focal bead, the bead cap from inside to outside, the saucer, and the fire-polished bead.

2 Use the chain-, and round-nose pliers and the wire cutters to make a wrapped loop (see page 21) wide enough to slide over the cord ends.

3 String the dangle on the leather necklace.

Helixa Necklace

This smart-looking necklace is certainly versatile—polished enough to wear to the office, and elegant enough for evening wear. A Russian spiral technique is employed to make the rope that frames the focal bead. It can be a bit of a challenge for the first round or two, but once you've mastered the rhythm of the stitch, it's a snap.

Materials

1 green and blue glass 25 mm x 29 mm focal bead

2 green and blue 8 mm faceted cube beads

1 tube of forest green size 8° seed beads

1 tube of cornflower blue size 11° seed beads

4 sterling silver 6 mm Bali-style daisy spacers

2 sterling silver 10 x 18 mm cones with a decorative pattern

1 sterling silver 16 mm S clasp

1 small spool of light blue beading thread

44 inches (1.1 m) of .010 beading wire

6 inches (15.2 cm) of 20-gauge sterling silver wire

Tools

Scissors

Size 10 or 12 beading needle

Wire cutters

Chain-nose pliers

Round-nose pliers

Beading wire cutters

Finished Length

18 inches (45.7 cm)

Creating the Ropes

1 Use the needle, thread, and seed beads to stitch two 8¼-inch (21.0 cm) lengths of Russian spiral rope (see page 30). Set the ropes aside.

Preparing the Stringing Components

2 Use the wire cutters to cut the sterling silver wire into two 3-inch (7.6 cm) pieces. Use the chain- and round-nose pliers to make a wrapped loop (see page 21) at the end of each wire. Set them aside.

3 Use the wire cutters to cut the beading wire into two 22-inch (55.9 cm) pieces. Set them aside.

Stringing the Necklace

4 Use a figure-eight knot (see page 25) to tie one end of one length of the beading wire to one of the wrapped loops, leaving a 3-inch (7.6 cm) tail. Repeat to attach the other length of beading wire, so you end up with two wires attached to one wrapped loop.

5 As you look down the center of one of the ropes, notice that the first round forms a circle of beads. Pass the end of one of the beading wires through these beads in one direction. Pass the end of the other beading wire through the same beads in the opposite direction. Pass both wires down through the rope and out the other end.

6 Repeat step 4 to pass the beading wires through the circle of beads at the other end of the rope. Pull the wires snug, but not tight enough to kink the rope. Use both wires to tie several square knots (see page 25) to secure the rope in place.

7 Use both wire ends to string on one daisy spacer, one cube bead, one daisy spacer, and the focal bead. Snug the beads and use both wires to make several square knots. String on one daisy spacer,

one cube bead, and one more daisy spacer. Slide the beads over the knots.

8 Repeat step 4 to attach the second spiral rope.

9 Repeat step 3 to attach the beading wires to the second wrapped loop. Be sure to keep the beading wire, ropes, and beads snug, but not tight enough to kink the rope.

10 Weave the loose ends of the beading wire back into the rope. Use the wire cutters to trim any excess beading wire.

Completing the Core Strand

11 String on one cone, from inside to outside, on one of the wrapped loop wires.

12 Tighten the cone against the beadwork and use the chain- and round-nose pliers to make a wrapped loop that attaches to one half of the S clasp (see Making a Core Strand, page 23).

13 Repeat steps 10 and 11 to complete the other side of the necklace.

Spring Buds Necklace

The crystals and pears in this spiral cord necklace evoke newly-budded flowers on a spring vine. The spiral ropes frame a sensational lampworked glass focal bead that features a spiral of its own.

Preparing the Components

1 Use the wire cutters to cut the gold-filled wire into two 3-inch (7.6 cm) pieces.

2 Use the chain- and round-nose pliers to form a wrapped loop (see page 21) at one end of each wire. Set them aside.

Stringing the Core Strand

3 Place a clip 3 inches (7.6 cm) from one end of the beading wire. String 63 size 6° seed beads, one bead cap from the outside in, the focal bead, one bead cap from the inside out, and 63 size 6° seed beads.

4 Check the design and make any adjustments. Make sure there is an equal amount of bare beading wire on each side of the strand.

Materials

1 topaz AB 25 mm x 35 mm lampworked glass focal bead

97 light sapphire 6 mm crystal round beads

30 light rose 4 mm x 6 mm top-drilled freshwater pearl beads

126 gold size 6° hex-cut seed beads

10 grams of transparent light amethyst size 11° seed beads

2 gold-filled 6 mm x 10 mm Bali-style bead caps (or sized to fit the focal bead)

2 gold-filled 10 mm x 20 mm Bali-style cones

1 gold-filled 30-mm S clasp with an amethyst pearl inlay

1 spool of beading thread to match the beads

25 inches (63.5 cm) of .010-inch (.025 cm) flexible beading wire

6 inches (15.2 cm) of 20-gauge gold-filled wire

Tools

Wire cutters

Chain-nose pliers

Round-nose pliers

2 bead clips

Size 10 beading needle

Finished Length

18¾ inches (46.0 cm)

Spring Buds Necklace

5   Use a figure-eight knot (see
page 25) to tightly tie one
end of the beading wire to one of
the wrapped loops. Snug the
beads and repeat to attach the
other end of the necklace to the
second wrapped loop. If possible,
pass the beading wire back
through the beads on the strand.
Trim any excess beading wire. Set
the strand aside.

Stitching the Strand

6   Cut a 3-foot (.9 cm) length of
the thread, pass it through the
needle, double it, and make a knot
at the end. Tie the end of the thread
to one of the wrapped loops.

7   Work a simple spiral (see
page 28) down the core
strand. Work 41 loops using three
size 11° beads, one crystal, and
three size 11° beads in each loop.
The loops should total 4½ inches
(11.4 cm).

8   Continue to work a simple
spiral down the core strand,
this time making 15 loops using
three size 11° beads, one pearl
bead, and three size 11° beads in
each loop. The loops should total
1½ inches (3.8 cm).

9   Repeat step 7 to make six
loops.

10   Make a square knot (see
page 25) on the beading
wire. Pass through the bead cap
and focal bead and make another
square knot on the beading wire.
Pass through the bead cap.

11   Repeat steps 7 to 9 in reverse, adding thread as
needed (see page 28). Tie it off on
the wrapped loop at the end of
the strand.

Completing the Core Strand

12   String on one cone,
from inside to outside,
on one of the wrapped loop
wires.

13   Tighten the cone against
the beadwork and use
the chain- and round-nose pliers
to make a wrapped loop that attaches to one half of the box
clasp (see Making a Core Strand,
page 23).

14   Repeat steps 12 and 13
to complete the other
side of the necklace.

Carnival Jungle

The freeform peyote-stitched straps on this neck-lace look like they could be intricate footpaths for a jungle sprite. The stitching sets the tone for the jumble of colors surrounding this necklace's trio of focal beads.

Materials

1 violet, green, topaz, and black 30 mm polymer clay flat round focal bead with a jungle floral theme

2 matching 16 mm x 35 mm polymer clay flat oval focal beads

4 violet AB 13 mm pressed glass leaf beads

7 green 10 mm pressed glass leaf beads

4 topaz 12 mm pressed glass leaf beads

2 transparent green 8 mm pressed glass pyramid beads

7 amethyst 6 mm crystal bicone beads

6 peridot 6 mm crystal bicone beads

8 topaz 6 mm crystal bicone beads

48 assorted 3 mm to 4 mm accent beads for the fringe ends to match the other beads

23 peridot 4 mm cube beads

13 violet-lined clear 4 mm cube beads

1 tube of copper-lined amethyst size 5° triangle seed beads

1 tube of copper-lined topaz size 5° triangle seed beads

1 tube of silver-lined peridot size 5° triangle seed beads

1 tube of purple size 6° seed beads

1 tube of silver-lined peridot size 6° seed beads

10 grams each of frosted amethyst, silver-lined green, silver-lined topaz, and shiny black size 11° seed beads

3 grams of silver-lined green regular (size 11°) cylinder beads 2 sterling silver 10 mm x 18 mm cones with a floral design

27 inches (68.6 cm) of .014-inch (.036 cm) flexible beading wire

1 spool of beading thread to match the beads

1 sterling silver 15 mm S clasp to match the cones

6 inches (15.2 cm) of 20-gauge sterling silver wire

Tools

Wire cutters

Chain-nose pliers

Round-nose pliers

2 bead clips

Scissors

Size 10 beading needle

Finished Length

20½ inches (52.1 cm)

Preparing the Components

1 Use the wire cutters to cut the sterling silver wire into two 3-inch (7.6 cm) pieces.

2 Use the chain- and round-nose pliers to form a wrapped loop (see page 21) at one end of each wire. Set them aside.

Stringing the Core Strand

3 Place a clip on one end of the beading wire. String on one amethyst crystal bead, one oval focal bead, one peridot crystal bead, nineteen purple size 6° beads, one topaz crystal bead, the round focal bead, one peridot crys-

Carnival Jungle

tal bead, nineteen purple size 6° beads, one topaz crystal bead, one oval focal bead, and one amethyst crystal bead.

4 String on five inches (12.7 cm) of beads in preparation for freeform peyote stitch. Use whichever beads appeal to you, but try to vary their size, shape, and color, always using an odd number of beads in each segment. For the necklace shown, the core strand was strung as follows: nine peridot size 6° beads, nine topaz size 5° beads, five purple size 6° beads, nine topaz size 11° beads, five peridot cube beads, five topaz size 5° beads, seven topaz size 11° beads, and three peridot size 5° triangle beads . End with one pyramid bead. Place a clip on this end of the wire.

5 Remove the first clip. Repeat step 4 on the other side of the necklace, varying the bead segments so they don't match the first side. End with one pyramid bead.

6 Check the design and make any adjustments. Make sure there is an equal amount of bare beading wire on each side of the strand. Use a figure-eight knot (see page 25) to tie each end of the wire to a wrapped loop. If possible, weave the loose ends of the wire back into the core strand. Trim any excess wire.

Beading the Necklace

7 Cut a 3-foot (.9 cm) length of the thread, pass it through the needle, double it, and tie a knot in the end. Tie the end of the thread to one of the wrapped loops.

8 Work freeform peyote stitch down to the first crystal bead. Pass the needle through the crystal bead, the oval focal bead, and the next crystal bead.

9 String on four black size 11° beads, one small accent bead, and one black size 11° bead. Skip the last bead you strung and pass the needle back through the rest of the beads to create a simple fringe leg (see page 25). Pass the needle through the next purple size 6° bead down the core strand. Continue making fringe between each size 6° bead until you reach the round focal bead. When creating the fringe, start out with five-bead stems near the oval focal bead and increase to seven- or eight-bead stems as you reach the round focal bead. (If you are using a larger focal bead, you may want to make the fringe even longer.) Use size 11° beads of various colors for the stems and different small accent beads for the ends to create a random look.

10 Pass the needle through the round focal bead and the next crystal bead. Repeat steps 8 and 9 in reverse. Tie it off to the second wrapped loop.

11 Repeat steps 8 to 10 to make at least three sets of fringe. It will take at least five passes to finish the peyote-stitched sections.

12 Embellish the peyote-stitched sections using strands of various seed and accent beads. Begin by passing the needle through a bead near the end of a section. String on a strand of four to ten seed beads interspersed with one or two accent beads. Pass down through a bead on a different peyote-stitched section. You need not only work from the top of the strap, but may also wrap the seed/accent bead strands around the strap to create a spiraling look. Continue down the peyote-stitched section and then tie it off. Repeat on the other side of the necklace.

Completing the Core Strand

13 String on one cone, from inside to outside, on one of the wrapped loop wires.

14 Tighten the cone against the beadwork and use the chain- and round-nose pliers to make a wrapped loop that attaches to one half of the S clasp (see Making a Core Strand, page 23).

15 Repeat steps 13 and 14 to complete the other side of the necklace.

Vienna Waltz Necklace

This substantial necklace is created with bead loops inter-mixed with bead strands, making it look like a thick braid of beads. When shopping for beads, let the focal bead's colors dictate the accent beads' colors, and then have fun finding the most interesting types and shapes.

Preparing the Components

1 Use the wire cutters to cut the sterling silver wire into two 3-inch (7.6 cm) pieces.

2 Use the chain- and round-nose pliers to form a wrapped loop (see page 21) at one end of each wire. Set them aside.

Stringing the Core Strand

3 Place a clip 3 inches (7.6 cm) from one end of the beading wire. String on 8 inches (20.3 cm) of size 6° beads, one 9 mm x 12 mm rondelle bead, the focal bead, one 9 mm x 12 mm rondelle bead, and 8 inches (20.3 cm) of size 6° beads.

4 Check the design and make any adjustments. Make sure there is an equal amount of bare beading wire on each side of the strand.

5 Remove the clip from one end of the strand. Use a figure-eight knot (see page 25) to tightly tie one end of the beading wire to one of the wrapped loops. Snug the beads and repeat to attach the other end of the necklace to the second wrapped loop. If possible, pass the beading wire back through the beads on the strand. Trim any excess beading wire.

Materials

1 black, green, rose, and blue 18 mm x 50 mm focal bead with a floral design

18 assorted 15 mm to 20 mm glass accent beads to match the focal bead

30 assorted 12 mm to 15 mm top-drilled glass accent beads to match the focal bead 2 sterling silver 9 mm x 12 mm rondelle beads

30 assorted 8 mm to 10 mm glass accent beads to match the focal bead

36 assorted 6 mm glass accent beads to match the focal bead

1 tube of transparent blue AB size 6° seed beads

1 tube of transparent green-lined size 8° triangle beads

1 tube of transparent rose size 8° seed beads

1 tube of blue AB size 8° hex-but beads

1 tube each of green, rose, and blue size 11° seed beads

2 sterling silver 10 mm x 12 mm cones with a filigree design

1 sterling silver 22 mm S clasp to match the cones

1 spool of beading thread to match beads

27 inches (68.6 cm) of .014-inch (.036 cm) beading wire

6 inches (15.2 cm) of 20-gauge sterling silver wire

Tools

Wire cutters

Chain-nose pliers

Round-nose pliers

2 bead clips

Scissors

Size 10 beading needle

Finished Length

21 inches (53.3 cm)

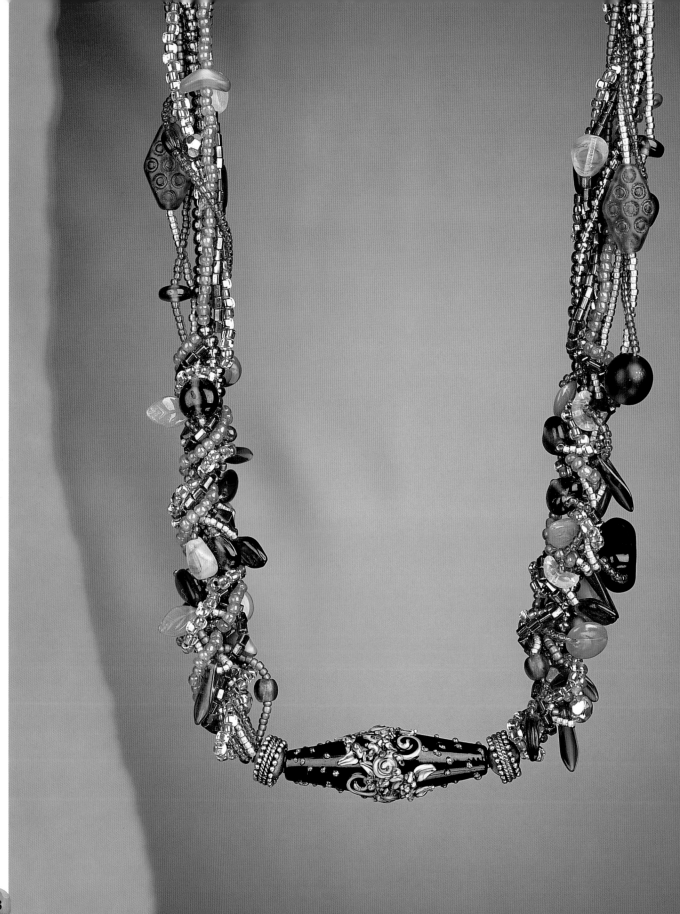

Vienna Waltz Necklace

Beading the Necklace

6 Cut a 3-foot (.9 m) length of the thread. Pass it through the needle, double it, and knot it. Tie the end of the thread to one of the wrapped loops.

7 String on 4 inches (10.2 cm) of size 8° triangle beads, interspersed with one large accent bead.

8 Keeping your thumb on the last bead strung to keep the beads snug against the wrapped loop, gently stretch the bead segment down the core strand. Pass the needle through the closest size 6° bead of the core strand.

9 String on 1 inch (2.5 cm) of size 8° triangle beads, and pass the needle through a nearby size 6° bead on the core strand to form a loop.

10 Repeat step 9 down the core strand until you reach the 9 mm x 12 mm rondelle bead.

11 Pass the needle through the first rondelle bead, the focal bead, and the next rondelle bead on the core strand.

12 Repeat steps 7 to 9 in reverse. Tie the end of the thread to the second wrapped loop.

13 Repeat steps 6 to12 twice more. On the first pass use size 8° hex beads and form 1¼-inch (3.2 cm) loops; on the second pass use rose size 8° beads and form 1½-inch (3.8 cm) loops. Keep the accent beads at different levels so they don't sit right next to each other on the necklace.

14 String on 8 inches (20.3 cm) of one color size 11° beads, adding small and/or medium accent beads at random intervals. Pass this strand through some of the loops, as well as over and under the core strand. Leave the strands loose or tight within the loops, depending on what feels right to you. If you make them really loose you may need to add more beads to the strand.

15 Pass the needle through the first silver rondelle bead, the focal bead, and the second silver rondelle bead.

16 Repeat step 14 and tie it off on the second wrapped loop.

17 Repeat steps 14 to 16 six more times, using the remaining size 11° bead colors. As you make additional strands, weave them through the last strands added as well as the loops on the core strand. When you work the last few strands, the space within the loops will get very tight. To help, string partial strands, pass the needle through the loop, and continue to string the strands.

Completing the Core Strand

18 String on one cone, from inside to outside, on one of the wrapped loop wires.

19 Tighten the cone against the beadwork and use the chain- and round-nose pliers to make a wrapped loop that attaches to one half of the S clasp (see Making a Core Strand, page 23).

20 Repeat steps 18 and 19 to complete the other side of the necklace.

Ancient Forest

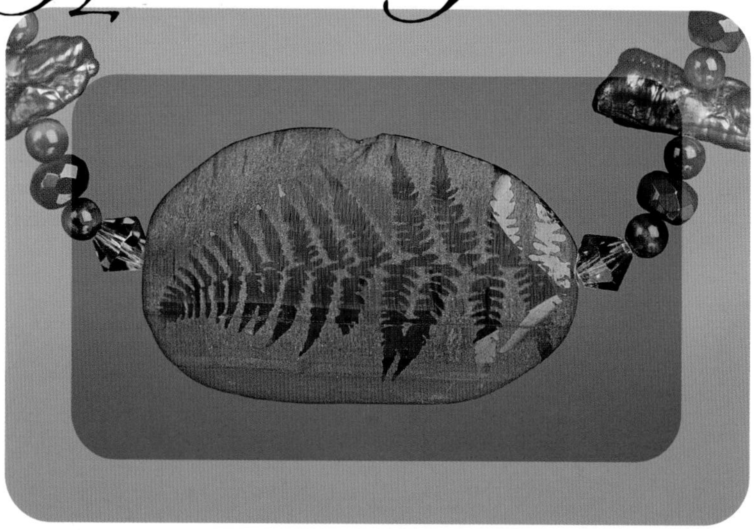

A drop of primordial tree sap seems to have captured a delicate fern from prehistoric woodlands. The image was actually etched into stone, but the stick pearls, amber crystals, and other semiprecious stone beads carry the ancient-feeling theme to the rest of this easily-strung piece.

Materials

1 semiprecious tiger eye 21 mm x 43 mm focal bead with a fern etching

6 burgundy 20 mm stick pearl beads

2 topaz 11 mm x 12 mm crystal polygon beads

2 semiprecious red jasper 10 mm round beads

6 burgundy 5 mm freshwater potato pearl beads

20 semiprecious tiger eye 4 mm x 6 mm faceted rondelles

12 topaz AB 6 mm crystal bicone beads

40 semiprecious tiger eye 4 mm round beads

2 sterling silver 10 mm x 18 mm cones with a floral design

1 sterling silver 15 mm S clasp

26 inches (66 cm) of .014-inch (.036 cm) flexible beading wire

6 inches (15.2 cm) of 20-gauge sterling silver wire

Tools

Wire cutters

Chain-nose pliers

Round-nose pliers

2 bead clips

Finished Length

20½ inches (53.0 cm)

Preparing the Components

1 Use the wire cutters to cut the sterling silver wire into two 3-inch (7.6 cm) pieces.

2 Use the chain- and round-nose pliers to form a wrapped loop (see page 21) at one end of each wire. Set them aside.

Stringing the Beads

3 Place a clip 3 inches (7.6 cm) from one end of the flexible beading wire.

4 String on one red jasper bead. String on a sequence of one tiger eye rondelle, one tiger eye round bead, one crystal bicone bead, one tiger eye round bead, one tiger eye rondelle, one tiger eye round bead, one potato pearl bead, and one tiger eye round bead. Repeat the sequence two more times.

Ancient Forest

5 String on one crystal bicone bead, one crystal polygon bead, and one crystal bicone bead. String on a sequence of one tiger eye round bead, one tiger eye rondelle, and one stick pearl bead. Repeat the sequence two more times. String on one tiger eye round bead, one tiger eye rondelle, one tiger eye round bead, and one crystal bicone bead.

6 String on the focal bead.

7 Repeat steps 3 to 5 in reverse.

8 Check the design and make any adjustments. Make sure there is an equal amount of bare beading wire on each side of the strand.

Completing the Core Strand

9 Remove the clip from one end of the strand. Use a figure-eight knot (see page 25) to tightly tie one end of the beading wire to one of the wrapped loops. Snug the beads and repeat to attach the other end of the necklace to the second wrapped loop. If possible, pass the beading wire back through the beads on the strand. Trim any excess beading wire.

10 String on one cone, from inside to outside, on one of the wrapped loop wires.

11 Tighten the cone against the beadwork and use the chain- and round-nose pliers to make a wrapped loop that attaches to one half of the S clasp (see Making a Core Strand, page 23).

12 Repeat steps 10 and 11 to complete the other side of the necklace.

Ella's Voice Necklace

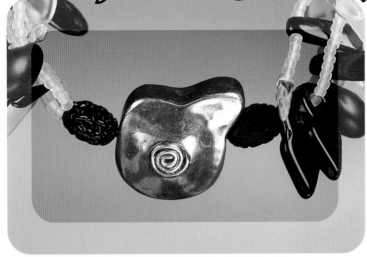

Like jazz music, this jewelry design is conducted in a syncopated rhythm. Instead of notes, however, the juxtaposition of different bead types, shapes, and sizes give this necklace its cool, sleek look.

Preparing the Components

1 Use the wire cutters to cut the sterling silver wire into two 3-inch (7.6 cm) pieces.

2 Use the chain- and round-nose pliers to form a wrapped loop (see page 21) at one end of each wire. Set them aside.

Stringing the Core Strand

3 Place a clip 3 inches (7.6 cm) from one end of the flexible beading wire. String on one clear saucer bead.

4 String on one black accent bead, one silver spacer, five clear seed beads, one silver spacer, and one clear accent bead.

5 String on 1½ inches (3.8 cm) of clear seed beads with two to three black cube beads interspersed.

6 String on one silver spacer, one black cube bead, one silver accent bead, and one black cube bead.

7 String on one silver spacer, five clear seed beads, one silver spacer, one clear accent bead, one black accent bead, one clear accent bead, one silver spacer, five clear seed beads, and one silver spacer.

8 String one bell flower bead from the wide end to the small end. String on the round focal bead, and one bell flower bead from the small end to the wide end.

9 String on 1¾ inches (4.5 cm) of clear seed beads interspersed with two to three top-drilled beads.

Materials

1 black and white 15 mm x 38 mm lampworked glass focal bead

1 black and white 17 mm lampworked glass round focal bead

1 hollow 20 mm x 27 mm sterling silver focal bead with a spiral design

4 black 12 mm x 16 mm pressed glass bell flower beads

2 clear AB 10 mm pressed glass saucer beads

2 black 10 mm pressed glass flat round beads

Assortment of 13 accent beads (6 black, 6 clear, 1 sterling silver), each 10 mm to 20 mm

50 top-drilled beads (25 clear, 25 black), each 8 mm to 18 mm long, including top-drilled teardrops, daggers, and slices

11 sterling silver 4.5 mm Bali-style daisy spacers

1 tube of black size 5° cube beads

1 tube of frosted clear size 11° seed beads

2 sterling silver 9 mm x 16 mm cones with a design

1 sterling silver 27 mm S clasp

1 spool of beading thread to match the beads

28 inches (71.1 cm) of .014-inch (.036 cm) flexible beading wire

6 inches (15.2 cm) of 20-gauge sterling silver wire

Tools

Wire cutters

Chain-nose pliers

Round-nose pliers

2 bead clips

Scissors

Size 10 beading needle

Finished Length

22 inches (55.9 cm)

Ella's Voice Necklace

10 String on one black 10 mm flat round bead, the silver focal bead, and one black 10 mm flat round bead.

11 Repeat steps 8 and 9 in reverse, this time using the large glass focal bead.

12 Repeat step 5.

13 String on one silver spacer, one black accent bead, one clear accent bead, one black accent bead, one silver spacer, five clear seed beads, one silver spacer, one clear accent bead, one black accent bead, and one clear saucer bead. Place a clip on this end of the wire.

14 Check the design and make any adjustments. Since this is an asymmetrical design, the sides will not match, but make sure you are happy with the bead placement.

15 Remove one of the clips and use a figure-eight knot (see page 25) to tie the wire end to one of the wrapped loops. Remove the other clip. Snug the beads and use a figure-eight knot to attach this end to the second wrapped loop. If possible, pass the beading wire back through the beads on the strand. Trim any excess beading wire. Set the strand aside.

Beading the Necklace

16 Cut a 3-foot (.9 m) length of the thread, pass it through the needle, double it, and tie a knot in the end. Tie the end of the thread to the wrapped loop on the side of the necklace you first started stringing.

17 Pass the needle through the clear saucer bead, the black accent bead, the clear accent bead, and the silver spacer. String on five clear seed beads and pass through the next spacer and clear accent bead.

18 Repeat step 5, making sure the cubes sit in different positions than the first strand. Pass the needle through the next silver spacer.

19 String on enough clear seed beads and one accent bead to reach the same length as the beads placed in step 6, and five clear seed beads. Pass the needle through the next silver spacer. String on five clear seed beads and pass the needle through the next silver spacer, clear accent bead, black accent bead, clear accent bead, and silver spacer. String on five clear seed beads and pass the needle through the next silver spacer, bell flower bead, focal bead, and bell flower bead.

20 Repeat step 9.

21 Pass the needle through the black flat round bead, silver focal bead, and black flat round bead.

22 Repeat step 9.

23 Pass the needle through the silver spacer, black accent bead, clear accent bead, black accent bead, and silver spacer. String on five clear seed beads and pass the needle through the next silver spacer and the rest of the beads to the end of the strand. Tie off the thread on the second wrapped loop.

24 Repeat steps 16 to 23 to add three more strands, always passing through the accent and focal beads, and adding additional seed bead strands.

Completing the Core Strand

25 String on one cone, from inside to outside, on one of the wrapped loop wires.

26 Tighten the cone against the beadwork and use the chain- and round-nose pliers to make a wrapped loop that attaches to one half of the S clasp (see Making a Core Strand, page 23).

27 Repeat steps 25 and 26 to complete the other side of the necklace.

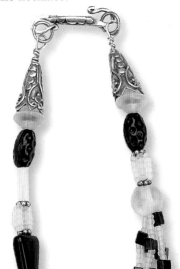

Orchid Rain Necklace

Materials

1 black 60 mm top-drilled glass flower focal bead

6 charolite 15mm round beads

10 rutilated quartz 12 mm x 15 mm faceted nugget beads

48 sterling silver 4 mm x 7 mm flat square beads with a design

1 sterling silver 12 mm box clasp with a garnet inset

14 sterling silver 2 mm x 2 mm crimp tubes

55 inches (1.4 m) of sterling silver-coated flexible beading wire

Tools

Wire cutters

Crimping pliers

Finished Length

18 inches (45.7 cm)

This piece by designer Mike Sherman features a detailed glass focal bead that seems to be drenched with rutilated quartz raindrops. Simple stringing is all you need to know to make this showstopper.

Stringing the Necklace Straps

1 Cut two 10-inch (25.4 cm) and five 7-inch (17.8 cm) pieces of wire. Set them aside.

2 Use one of the 10-inch (25.4 cm) pieces of wire to string one crimp tube and one half of the clasp. Pass the wire end back through the crimp tube, leaving a 1-inch (2.5 cm) tail. Snug the tube against the clasp and use crimping pliers to crimp the tube (see page 21). Trim the tail wire close to the tube.

3 String on 16 square beads. String on a sequence of one charolite bead and one square bead. Repeat the sequence twice more. String on one crimp tube.

4 Pass the wire end through the hole at the top of the focal bead. Pass the wire back through the tube. Leaving a 4 mm loop between the crimp tube and the focal bead, snug the beads and crimp the tube. Cut any excess wire.

5 Repeat steps 2 to 4 to make the other necklace strap.

Finishing the Necklace

6 String one crimp tube onto one of the 7-inch (17.8 cm) pieces of wire. Crimp the tube at the very end of the wire. Repeat this step to add crimp tubes to each of the other 7-inch (17.8 cm) wires.

7 String one quartz bead on each of the short wires.

8 String three square beads on one wire; string on one square bead on one wire; and string one square bead on one wire.

9 Gather all the short wires and pair the ends. Pass the wires through both of the wire loops created at the top of the focal bead.

10 Repeat steps 6 to 8 in reverse.

Mardi Gras Necklace

1 blue, green, and dichroic 33 mm lamp-worked glass flat round focal bead

4 transparent sapphire 8 mm x 12 mm pressed glass twisted flat oval beads

6 amethyst AB 7 mm faceted cube beads

6 transparent sapphire 7 mm pressed glass pyramid beads

8 sapphire 6 mm crystal bicone beads

6 light rose 6 mm crystal bicone beads

6 light yellow 6 mm crystal bicone beads

2 transparent blue-lined size 2° seed beads

6 transparent peach 5 mm cube beads

14 sapphire 4 mm crystal bicone beads

10 light yellow 4 mm crystal bicone beads

12 transparent hot pink-lined size

6° triangle beads

1 tube of transparent blue purple-lined size 6° triangle beads

1 tube of transparent yellow-lined size 6° seed beads

1 tube of blue silver-lined large (3.5 mm) cylinder beads

1 tube of peach size 8° hex-cut seed beads

1 tube of hot pink dyed size 8° seed beads

1 tube of pink regular (similar to size 11°) cylinder seed beads

1 tube of transparent yellow-lined size 11° seed beads

1 tube of dark blue silver-lined size 11° seed beads

2 sterling silver 10 mm x 14 mm scalloped cones with a design

1 sterling silver 23 mm S clasp with a citrine inlay

1 spool of beading thread to match the beads

22½ inches (57.2 cm) of .014-inch (.036 cm) flexible beading wire

6 inches (15.2 cm) of 20-gauge sterling silver wire

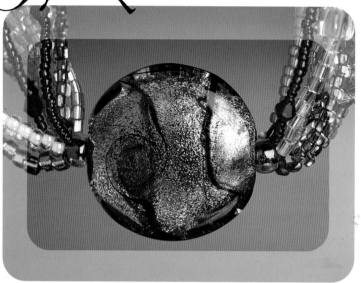

Party year round with this festive necklace made with multiple strands of seed, pressed glass, and crystal beads. It's an easy design to accomplish— just stringing all the way.

Tools

Wire cutters

Chain-nose pliers

Round-nose pliers

2 bead clips

Scissors

Size 10 beading needle

Finished Length

18 inches (46.0 cm)

Preparing the Components

1 Use the wire cutters to cut the sterling silver wire into two 3-inch (7.6 cm) pieces.

2 Use the chain- and round-nose pliers to form a wrapped loop (see page 21) at one end of each wire. Set them aside.

Stringing the Core Strand

3 Place a clip 3 inches (7.6 cm) from one end of the flexible beading wire. String on one faceted cube bead, one sapphire 6 mm crystal bead, and 21 yellow size 6° seed beads. String on a sequence of one sapphire 6 mm crystal bead,

Mardi Gras Necklace

one faceted cube bead, one sapphire 6 mm crystal bead, and 13 yellow size 6° seed beads. Repeat the sequence.

4 String on one size 2° seed bead, the focal bead, and one size 2° seed bead.

5 Repeat step 3 in reverse. Place a clip at this end of the strand.

6 Check the design and make any adjustments. Make sure there is an equal amount of bare beading wire on each side of the strand.

Stringing the Yellow Strands

7 Cut a 3-foot (.9 m) length of the thread and pass it through the needle. Double the thread and tie a knot in the end. Tie the knotted end of thread to one of the wrapped loops. Pass the needle through the 7 mm cube bead at the end of the core strand.

8 String on a sequence of 1 inch (2.5 cm) of yellow size 11° beads and one yellow 4 mm crystal beads. Repeat the sequence two more times. String on a sequence of 1 inch (2.5 cm) of yellow size 11° beads and one yellow 6 mm crystal bead. Repeat this sequence two more times. Note: There are going to be multiple strands with lots of crystals, so the seed bead measurements and crystal placements don't need to be exact. The strands should look like the crystals are randomly sprinkled throughout the necklace.

9 Pass the needle through the size 2° seed bead, the focal bead, and size 2° seed bead. Repeat step 8 in reverse and tie off onto the second wrapped loop.

10 Repeat steps 7 to 9, stringing yellow size 11° seed beads and yellow crystal beads. Use three 4 mm crystal beads and one 6 mm crystal bead for each side of the necklace, spacing them equally apart.

Stringing the Pink Strands

11 Repeat step 7. Pass the needle through the 6 mm crystal bead at the end of the core strand. String on three pink size 8° seed beads. String on a sequence of one pink size 6° triangle seed bead and 11 pink size 8° seed beads. Repeat the sequence five more times.

12 Pass the needle through the size 2° seed bead, the focal bead, and the next size 2° seed bead. Repeat step 11 in reverse and tie off onto the second wrapped loop.

13 Repeat step 7. String on a sequence of 1½ inches (3.8 cm) of pink cylinder beads, one pink size 8° seed bead, one rose 6 mm crystal bead, and one pink size 8° seed bead. Repeat the sequence two more times. String on ¾ inch (1.9 cm) of pink cylinder beads.

14 Pass the needle through the size 2° seed bead, the focal bead, and the next size 2° seed bead. Repeat step 13 in reverse and tie off on the second wrapped loop.

15 Repeat step 7. String on a sequence of 2 inches (5.1 cm) of peach hex beads and one peach cube bead. Repeat the sequence two more times. String on 1 inch (2.5 cm) of peach hex beads.

16 Pass the needle through the size 2° seed bead, the focal bead, and the next size 2° seed bead. Repeat step 15 in reverse and tie off on the second wrapped loop.

Stringing the Blue Strands

17 Repeat step 7. String on a sequence of 15 blue cylinder beads and one blue pyramid bead. Repeat the sequence two more times. String on seven blue cylinder beads.

18 Pass the needle through the size 2° seed bead, the focal bead, and the next size 2° seed bead. Repeat step 17 in reverse and tie off on the second wrapped loop.

19 Repeat step 7. String on a sequence of 21 blue triangle beads, one sapphire 6mm crystal bead, one twisted flat oval bead, and one sapphire 6 mm crystal bead. Repeat the sequence. String on 11 blue triangle beads.

20 Pass the needle through the size 2° seed bead, the focal bead, and the next size 2° seed bead. Repeat step 19 in reverse and tie off on the second wrapped loop.

21 Repeat step 7. String on a sequence of 1¼ inches (3.2 cm) of blue size 11° seed beads and one sapphire 4 mm crystal bead. Repeat the sequence three more times. String on five blue size 11° seed beads.

22 Pass the needle through the size 2° seed bead, the focal bead, and the next size 2° seed bead. Repeat step 21 in reverse and tie off on the second wrapped loop.

23 Repeat step 7, stringing blue size 11° seed beads and sapphire 4 mm crystal beads. Use three crystal beads for each side of the necklace, spacing them equally apart.

Completing the Core Strand

24 Remove the clip from one end of the strand. Use a figure-eight knot (see page 25) to tightly tie one end of the beading wire to one of the wrapped loops. Snug the beads and repeat to attach the other end of the necklace to the second wrapped loop. If possible, pass the beading wire back through the beads on the strand. Trim any excess beading wire.

25 String on one cone, from inside to outside, on one of the wrapped loop wires.

26 Tighten the cone against the beadwork and use the chain- and round-nose pliers to make a wrapped loop that attaches to one half of the S clasp (see Making a Core Strand, page 23).

27 Repeat steps 18 and 19 to complete the other side of the necklace.

Iris Rhapsody Necklace

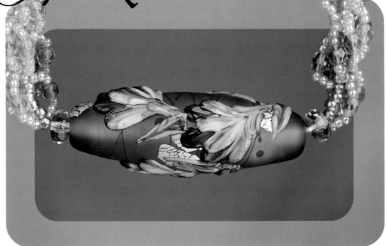

The lampworked glass focal bead at the center of this necklace has a delicate look, but it's really quite heavy. This design maintains the lacy and light look of the bead, but its construction, which uses both the core strand and simple spiral techniques, makes the necklace very sturdy.

Materials

1 violet, lavender, green, gold, and black 17 mm x 48 mm focal bead with a floral design

4 violet 12 mm bell flower beads

14 violet 6 mm crystal bicone beads

8 lavender 4 mm x 7 mm crystal rondelle beads

2 dichroic-lined clear size 2° beads

2 green 4 mm faceted fire-polished round beads

28 lavender 3 mm faceted fire-polished round beads

38 lavender AB size 8° seed beads

1 tube each of silver-lined light amethyst and cornflower size 11° seed beads

2 sterling silver 13 mm x 25 mm cones with a floral design

1 sterling silver 25 mm S clasp to match the cones

1 spool of beading thread to match the beads

26 inches (66 cm) of .014-inch (.036 cm) flexible beading wire

6 inches (15.2 cm) of 20-gauge sterling silver wire loops

Tools

Wire cutters

Chain-nose pliers

Round-nose pliers

2 bead clips

Scissors

Size 10 beading needle

Finished Length

19½ inches (49.5 cm)

Preparing the Components

1 Use the wire cutters to cut the sterling silver wire into two 3-inch (7.6 cm) pieces.

2 Use the chain- and round-nose pliers to form a wrapped loop (see page 21) at one end of each wire. Set them aside.

Stringing the Core Strand

3 Place a clip 3 inches (7.6 cm) from one end of the beading wire. String one flower bead from the top down. String on a sequence of nineteen amethyst size 11° beads and one crystal bicone bead. Repeat the sequence two more times. String on 19 amethyst size 11° beads.

4 String on one green fire-polished bead, one size 2° bead, one flower bead from the top down, 19 size 8° beads, and one crystal rondelle bead.

5 String on the focal bead.

6 Repeat steps 3 and 4 in reverse.

7 Check the design and make any adjustments. Make sure there is an equal amount of bare beading wire on each side of the strand.

8 Remove the clip from one end of the strand. Use a figure-eight knot (see page 25) to tightly tie one end of the beading wire to one of the wrapped loops. Snug the beads and repeat to attach the other end of the necklace to the second wrapped loop. If possible, pass the beading wire back through the beads on the strand. Trim any excess beading wire.

Beading the Necklace

9 Cut a 3-foot (.9 m) length of the thread. Pass it through the needle, double it, and knot it. Tie the end of the thread to one of the wrapped loops.

10 String on 31 amethyst size 11° beads. String on a sequence of one rondelle and 27 amethyst size 11° beads. Repeat the sequence. Pass the needle through the green fire-polished bead, the size 2° bead, and the bell flower bead.

11 Work a simple spiral (see page 28) down the segment of size 8° beads. Make one loop by stringing three cornflower size 11° beads, one lavender fire-polished bead, and three cornflower size 11° beads. Make 14 loops.

12 Pass the needle through the rondelle bead, the focal bead, and the rondelle bead.

13 Repeat steps 9 and 10 in reverse. Tie the thread onto the second wrapped loop.

14 Start a new thread on one of the wrapped loops. String on a sequence of 13 amethyst size 11° beads and one crystal bicone bead. Repeat the sequence three more times. String on seven amethyst size 11° beads. Pass the needle through the beads on the core strand until you reach the second green fire-polished bead.

15 Repeat the stringing sequence in step 13 in reverse. Tie the end of the thread to the second wrapped loop.

Completing the Core Strand

16 String on one cone, from inside to outside, on one of the wrapped loop wires.

17 Tighten the cone against the beadwork and use the chain- and round-nose pliers to make a wrapped loop that attaches to one half of the S clasp (see Making a Core Strand, page 23).

18 Repeat steps 15 and 16 to complete the other side of the necklace.

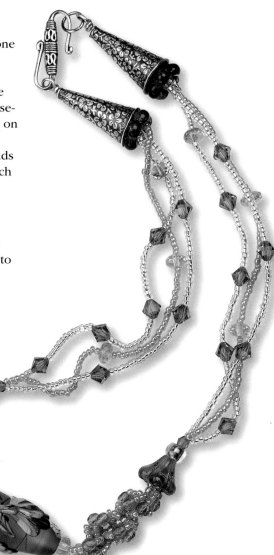

Sakura Necklace

The elegant geisha-shaped focal bead featured in this necklace is surrounded by equally rich freshwater pearls and handmade washi paper beads. The bead combination creates an understated, yet joyous celebration.

Stringing the Beads

1 Place a clip 3 inches (7.5 cm) from one end of the beading wire. String on a sequence of one washi bead, one bicone bead, five pearl beads, and one bicone bead. Repeat the sequence. String on one cube bead, one polygon bead, and one cube bead.

2 String on a sequence of one bicone bead, five pearl beads, one bicone bead, and one washi bead. Repeat the sequence. String on one bicone bead and three pearl beads.

Materials

1 black, white, and burgundy 33 mm x 55 mm lampworked glass geisha-shaped focal bead

2 transparent fuchsia dichroic-lined 10 mm x 14 mm lampworked glass polygon beads

8 gold, terra cotta, and burgundy 8 mm washi paper round beads

4 topaz 6 mm crystal cube beads

19 black 6 mm crystal bicone beads

46 burgundy 6 mm freshwater potato pearl beads

2 transparent dichroic-lined 4 mm x 6 mm lampworked glass beads

1 burgundy size 11° seed bead

1 sterling silver 10 mm x 18 mm cone clasp

30 inches (76.2 cm) of .014-inch (.036 cm) flexible beading wire

Tools

2 bead clips

Chain-nose pliers

Finished Length

19½ inches (49.5 cm)

Sakura Necklace

3 String on one 4 mm x 6 mm bead, the focal bead, one 4 mm x 6 mm bead, one bicone bead, and the seed bead. Skipping the seed bead, pass the wire back through all the beads you've strung in this step (see figure 1).

4 Repeat steps 1 and 2 in reverse. Place a clip at this end of the strand.

5 Check the design and make any adjustments. Make sure there is an equal amount of bare beading wire on each side of the strand.

Connecting the Clasp

6 Remove the clip from one end of the wire. Use a figure-eight knot (see page 25) to tightly tie the wire end to the spring for one half of the clasp. If possible, pass the wire back through beads on the strand. Trim any excess wire.

7 Use the chain-nose pliers to put the spring into the cone clasp until you feel it snap into place (see figure 2). Note: Once you place the spring, you won't be able to get it out again except by cutting it.

8 Repeat steps 6 and 7 to complete the other side of the necklace.

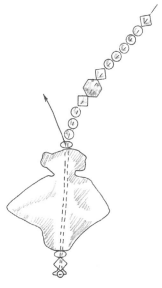

Figure 1

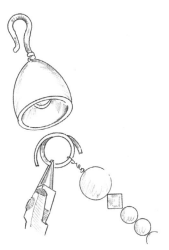

Figure 2

Wavy Sea Bracelet

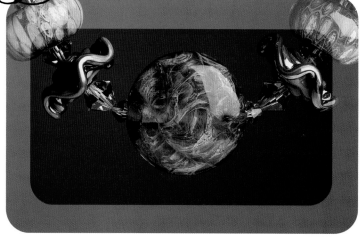

Like snowflakes, this lampworked glass focal bead is likely unique. Rather than trying to find an exact match, look for one flat enough to lay comfortably against the wrist.

Stringing the Beads

1 Cut 2 feet (61.0 cm) of the thread. Pass it through the needle and double it. Place a clip 6 inches (15.2 cm) from one end of the thread.

2 String on one seed bead, three 4 mm crystal beads, one 6 mm x 10 mm bead, three 4 mm crystal beads, one 5 mm crystal bead, one 5 mm x 12 mm bead, one 5 mm crystal bead, one 6 mm crystal bead, one ruffled bead, one 6 mm crystal bead, one 6 mm x 16 mm bead, one 6 mm crystal bead, one ruffled bead, one 6 mm crystal bead, and one 4 mm crystal bead.

3 String on the focal bead.

4 Repeat step 2 in reverse and place a clip at the end of the thread. Check the design and make any adjustments. Slide the beads toward the center of the thread and move the clips to get rid of any slack.

5 Remove the clip at one end of the strand. Pass the needle through the loop on the lobster clasp. String on one seed bead.

Materials

1 blue and green 20 mm lampworked glass focal bead

4 blue and green 6 mm x 16 mm ruffled lampworked glass beads

2 blue and green 5 mm x 12 mm lampworked glass rondelles

2 navy 6 mm x 10 mm lampworked glass rondelles

8 light emerald 6 mm crystal bicone beads

4 light emerald 5 mm crystal bicone beads

12 light emerald 4 mm crystal bicone beads

3 matte clear silver-lined size 11° seed beads

1 spool of beading thread to match the beads

1 sterling silver 6 mm soldered jump ring

1 sterling silver 12 mm lobster clasp

Tools

Scissors

Size 10 beading needle

2 bead clips

Finished Length

7½ inches (19.1 cm)

Securing the Thread

6 Pass the needle back through a few beads on the strand. Tie a square knot (see page 25) and pass it through the next few beads, pulling the thread tight to hide the knot within the beads. Repeat down the length of the strand.

7 When you reach the end of the strand, remove the bead clip. Slide the beads toward the lobster clasp to get rid of any slack in the strand.

8 Remove the needle from the working thread and thread it on the tail. String on the jump ring and pass it back through the last few beads of the strand.

9 Repeat step 6 to secure the thread. Tie it off.

Dancer's Song Necklace

Materials

1 red, black, and gold 25 mm x 33 mm lampworked glass focal bead

2 crimson 10 mm glass round beads

1 ruby 15 mm crystal briolette bead

1 burnt orange 15 mm disk pendant

10 black 8 mm x 13 mm two-holed pressed glass beads

2 gold-filled 5 mm x 8 mm saucer beads

2 black 4 mm x 6 mm saucer beads

10 red 3 mm faceted fire-polished beads

110 gold, red, and black accent beads in an assortment of types and shapes, sizes 2 mm to 10 mm

1 tube of gold size 11° seed beads

2 gold-filled 15 mm x 18 mm bell cones with a striated design

1 gold-filled 30 mm S clasp with a spiral design

1 spool of beading thread to match the beads

48 inches (1.2 m) of .010-inch (.025 cm) flexible beading wire

6 inches (15.2 cm) of 20-gauge gold-filled wire

Tools

Wire cutters

Chain-nose pliers

Round-nose pliers

Finished Length

28 inches (71.1 cm)

This multi-strand necklace is like music for a grand ballet. Simple strings of seed beads move gracefully through unusual two-holed beads. Try substituting a different color palette and you'll compose a piece of jewelry that's sung in a brand new key.

Preparing the Components

1 Use the wire cutters to cut the gold-filled wire into two 3-inch (7.6 cm) pieces.

2 Use the chain- and round-nose pliers to form a wrapped loop (see page 21) at one end of each wire. Set them aside.

Stringing the Core Strand

3 Use a figure-eight knot (see page 25) to tightly tie one end of the beading wire to one of the wrapped loops, leaving a 3-inch (7.6 cm) tail.

4 String on one crimson 10 mm round bead, one black saucer bead, and 2½ inches (6.4 cm) of seed beads interspersed with randomly-placed accent beads. Note: The necklace is made up of several of seed and accent bead segments. In order to end up with enough accent beads to complete the necklace, each segment should average about three accent beads. 5. String on one two-holed bead through the left hole and 1½ inches (3.8 cm) of seed beads interspersed

with accent beads. Repeat this sequence, always stringing on one two-holed bead followed by segments of seed and accent beads. The segment lengths are as follows: 2¼ inches (5.7 cm), 1¾ inches (4.5 cm), 1¼ inches (3.2 cm), and 1½ inches (3.8 cm).

5 String on one red 3 mm fire-polished bead, one gold saucer bead, the focal bead, one gold saucer bead, one red 3 mm fire-polished bead, 1½ inches (3.8 cm) of seed beads, and the disk pendant. String on three seed beads and pass the wire back through the fourth-to-last seed bead of the 1½-inch (3.8 cm) seed bead length that you just strung. Continue passing the wire back through all the seed beads of the strand. Tie a square knot (see page 25) and trim the wire so it has a ¾ inch (1.9 cm) tail. Tuck the tail to hide it inside the focal bead.

6 Repeat steps 3 to 6 to make the other side of the necklace. For this side, you'll tie onto the other wrapped loop, and when you come to the bottom to create the fringe leg, use the briolette bead to finish the strand. Set the strand aside.

Stringing the Other Strands

7 Cut a 3-foot (.9 m) length of the thread, pass it through the needle, double it, and tie a knot at the end. Tie the end of the thread to one of the wrapped loops.

8 Pass through the red 10 mm round bead and black saucer bead at the end of the strand. String on 2½ inches (6.4 cm) of seed beads and accent beads as

you did for the core strand, being sure to place the accent beads in different places as those on the core strand. Pass the needle through the right hole of the first two-hole bead you placed on the core strand. Continue adding seed beads and accent beads to match the segments added in the core strand, always passing through the right hole of the two-holed beads.

9 Repeat step 6, except this time, when you reach the end of the fringe leg, string on one 10 mm accent bead and one seed bead. Pass the needle back through the rest of the seed beads, saucer bead, focal bead, saucer bead, and the last red 3 mm that you strung.

10 Using the same thread and working in the opposite direction, add seed beads and accent beads in segments as you did before, always passing the needle through the right side of the two-holed bead. When you reach the wrapped loop you originally started with, tie it off.

11 Repeat steps 8 and 9, this time passing through the left hole of the two-holed beads.

12 When you turn the needle around to work back up the other side of the necklace, pass through the left hole of the two-holed beads (see figure 1). When you reach the wrapped loop, tie it off.

13 Repeat steps 8 to 11, this time passing through the right hole of the two-holed beads, to make two more strands on this side of the necklace. The com-

pleted stringing should leave you with four strands on each side of the necklace and five fringe legs. Set the necklace aside.

Completing the Core Strand

14 String on one cone, from inside to outside, on one of the wrapped loop wires.

15 Tighten the cone against the beadwork and use the chain- and round-nose pliers to make a wrapped loop that attaches to one half of the S clasp (see Making a Core Strand, page 23).

16 Repeat steps 15 and 16 to complete the other side of the necklace.

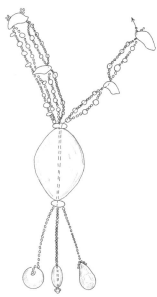

Figure 1

Eclectique Necklace

You get a little bit of everything when you bead this colorful necklace—freeform peyote stitches, stringing, seed beads, crystals, pearls, pressed glass, and silver! Wearing it can be just as versatile—it'll look fabulous whether you're dressing up or down.

Preparing the Components

1 Use the wire cutters to cut the sterling silver wire into two 3-inch (7.6 cm) pieces.

2 Use the chain- and round-nose pliers to form a wrapped loop (see page 21) at one end of each wire. Set them aside.

Stringing the Core Strand

3 Place a clip 3 inches (7.6 cm) from one end of the beading wire. String one amethyst 8 mm faceted cube bead and 7¼ inches (18.4 cm) of red size 11° seed beads with 10 pearl beads interspersed throughout the strand.

4 String on one pear bead, one crystal cube bead, one pearl bead, the focal bead, one pearl bead, one crystal cube bead, and one red pearl bead.

5 String the second side of the necklace in preparation for freeform peyote stitch. Use whichever beads appeal to you, but try to vary size, shape, and color, and always use an odd number of beads. For the project shown, the stringing sequence is 1 inch (2.5 cm) of blue size 11° seed beads; ½ inch (1.3 cm) of green size 8° seed beads; 1 inch (2.5 cm) of amethyst size 11° seed beads, one sapphire 8 mm faceted cube bead; ¾ inch (1.9 cm) of amethyst size 11° seed beads; ¾ inch (1.9 cm) of blue size 6° seed beads; 1¼

Materials

1 red, blue, and dichroic 26 mm lamp-worked glass focal bead

2 amethyst 8 mm faceted cube beads

1 sapphire 8 mm faceted cube bead

2 crimson 8 mm crystal cube beads

5 red 8 mm pressed glass bell flowers

4 crimson 6 mm faceted fire-polished beads

Approximately 55 burgundy 5 mm freshwater potato pearl beads

10 grams of silver-lined blue size 6° seed beads

10 grams of transparent crimson size 8° hex-cut seed beads

1 gram of transparent peridot size 8° seed beads

20 grams of transparent red size 11° seed beads

10 grams of purple-lined transparent blue size 11° seed beads

10 grams of transparent amethyst size 11° seed beads

2 sterling silver 10 mm x 20 mm cones with Bali-style designs

1 sterling silver 15 mm box clasp with garnet inlay

26 inches (66 cm) of .010-inch (.025 cm) flexible beading wire

1 spool of beading thread to match the beads

6 inches (15.2 cm) of 20-gauge sterling silver wire

Tools

Wire cutters

Chain-nose pliers

Round-nose pliers

2 bead clips

Scissors

Size 10 beading needle

Finished Length

20 inches (51.0 cm)

inches (3.2 cm) crimson hex beads; ½ inch (1.3 cm) of blue size 11° seed beads; ¾ inch (1.9 cm) of amethyst size 11° seed beads; ½ inch (1.3 cm) of peridot size 8° seed beads; ½ inch (1.3 cm) of blue size 6° seed beads; and ⅜ inch (0.9 cm) of crimson hex beads. Place a clip at this end of the wire.

6 Check the design and make any adjustments. Slide the beads toward the center of the thread and move the clips to get rid of any slack.

7 Remove the clip from one end of the strand. Use a figure-eight knot (see page 25) to tightly tie one end of the beading wire to one of the wrapped loops. Snug the beads and repeat to attach the other end of the necklace to the second wrapped loop. If possible, pass the beading wire back through the beads on the strand. Trim any excess beading wire. Set the strand aside.

Beading the Necklace

8 Cut a 3-foot (90.0 cm) length of the thread. Pass it through the needle, double it, and knot it. Tie the end of the thread to the wrapped loop at the end of the freeform peyote-stitch stringing sequence.

9 Work freeform peyote stitch down the strand until you reach the first seed bead strung on this side of the necklace.

10 String on seven red size 11° seed beads and, skipping the pearl bead, pass the needle through the crystal cube bead. String on four to seven red size 11° seed beads and one pearl bead. Pass the needle through the focal bead. String on one pearl bead and four to seven red size 11° seed beads. Pass the needle through the next crystal cube (see figure 1).

11 String on a 7 1/4-inch (18.4 cm) strand of red size 11° seed beads, again interspersing the strand with pearl beads, this time placing them at different locations than the first strand. Pass the needle through the 8 mm bead at the end of the strand and tie the thread off onto the wrapped loop.

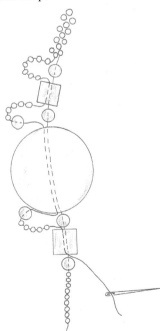

Figure 1

12 Repeat steps 8 to 11 to add strands to one side of the necklace and freeform peyote stitch to the other. Once you've completed five red seed bead strands on the stranded side of the necklace, add two strands of inter-mixed blue size 11° and green size 8° seed beads, adding the bell flowers and fire-polished beads at random intervals.

13 The peyote-stitched side of the necklace may require more rows than the stranded side—just simply add thread and beaded rows to this side of the necklace only until you are pleased with the design. Embellish these rows with bell flowers, pearl beads, and fire-polished beads to balance it with the other side of the necklace. Once you are pleased with the design, tie off all threads.

Completing the Core Strand

14 String on one cone, from inside to outside, on one of the wrapped loop wires.

15 Tighten the cone against the beadwork and use the chain- and round-nose pliers to make a wrapped loop that attaches to one half of the clasp (see Making a Core Strand, page 23).

16 Repeat steps 14 and 15 to complete the other side of the necklace.

Nonpareil Bracelet

Like the little candy buttons with white dotted decorations, this bracelet is especially sweet. It features three matching beads to space the weight evenly around the wrist—an important consideration when designing bracelets with focal beads.

Materials

3 black and white 17 mm lampworked glass lentil-shaped focal beads with a floral design

8 black 6 mm crystal bicone beads

11 white 5 mm freshwater pearl top-drilled beads

1 tube of black size 8° seed beads

1 tube of white size 11° seed beads

1 tube of black size 11° seed beads

1 black 15 mm shank button to compliment the focal beads

1 spool of black beading thread

1 spool of white beading thread

Tools

Scissors

Size 10 beading needle

Finished Length

7¾ inches (19.7 cm)

Stringing the Core Strand

1 Cut a 3-foot (90.0 cm) length of the black thread, pass it through the needle, and double it. Place a clip 6 inches (15.2 cm) from the end of the thread.

2 String on one crystal bead, nine size 8° beads, one crystal bead, one focal bead, one crystal bead, five size 8° beads, one crystal, one focal bead, one crystal bead, five size 8° beads, one crystal bead, one focal bead, one crystal bead, and nine size 8° beads.

Stitching the Bracelet

3 Work peyote stitch (see page 26) down the first nine-bead segment. Pass the needle through the crystal bead, the focal bead, and following crystal bead. Work peyote stitch down the next segment of seed beads. Continue to the end.

4 Repeat step 3 until you've made five rows of peyote stitch up and down the bracelet. Tie off the thread.

Nonpareil Bracelet

Making the Button/Loop Clasp

5 String on one crystal bead, 13 black size 11° beads, and the button. Pass the needle back through a size 8° bead at the end of the bracelet to seat the button. Pass the needle through the loop of beads again to reinforce it and then tie it off.

6 Remove the clip at the other end of the bracelet and thread a needle on the tail. String on one crystal and enough size 11° beads (about 27) to fit snugly around the button. Pass the needle back through the crystal and weave back through the beads again to reinforce it. Tie it off.

Embellishing the Bracelet

7 Cut a 1-foot (30.5 cm) length of the white thread, pass it through the needle, and double it. Attach the thread to the beadwork at one end of the bracelet so you exit from the first size 8° bead of the peyote-stitched segment. You'll want your needle to exit toward the focal beads.

8 String on five white size 11° beads, one pearl bead, five white size 11° beads, one pearl bead, and three white size 11° beads. Pass the needle through the first focal bead, the next crystal, and the first size 8° bead at the beginning of this peyote-stitched segment.

9 String on a sequence of five white size 11° beads and one pearl bead. Repeat the sequence three more times. String on three white size 11° beads. Pass the needle through the second and third size 8° beads on the next peyote-stitched segment. (The strand will loop over the middle focal bead).

10 String on a sequence of five white size 11° beads and one pearl bead. Repeat the sequence two more times. String on five white size 11° beads. Pass the needle through the second and third size 8° beads on the final peyote-stitched segment.

11 String on three white size 11° beads, one pearl bead, and five white size 11° beads. Pass the needle back through the last two size 8° beads of the last segment. String on two white size 11° beads, one pearl bead, and two white size 11° beads. Tie it off.

Shaman Necklace

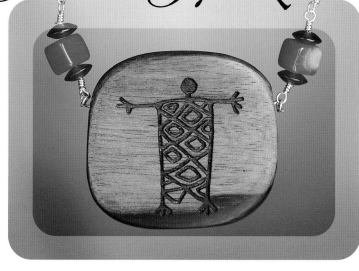

A voice from the past graces this necklace designed by Lora LaFhae. Because the focal bead is made of thin tiger ebony wood it's extremely light, so connecting it with thin wire and silk cord is all that's necessary to keep the necklace strong and beautiful.

Making the Beaded Chain

1 Cut sixteen 4-inch (10.2 cm) lengths of wire and one 5-inch (12.7 cm) length. Set them aside.

2 Use the chain- and round-nose pliers to make a wrapped loop (see page 21) at the end of one of the 4-inch (10.2 cm) wires. String on one horn bead, one coral bead, and one horn bead. Make another wrapped loop to secure the beads. Set the beaded link aside.

3 Use another piece of 4-inch (10.2 cm) wire to make a wrapped loop, but before completing the wrap, connect it to the previously-made link. String on one horn bead, one coral bead, and one horn bead. Make another wrapped loop to secure the beads.

4 Repeat step 3 until you have a chain of four beaded links.

Materials

1 tiger ebony 38 mm x 42 mm flat square focal bead with a shaman symbol

6 tiger ebony 6 mm cube beads

8 apple coral 6 mm cube beads

8 horn 6 mm saucer beads

4 tiger ebony 5 mm round beads

20 gold-filled 2 mm seamless round beads

2 gold-filled knot cups

2 gold-filled 2 mm x 2 mm crimp tubes

2 gold-filled 6 mm split rings

1 gold-filled toggle clasp with a rope design

28 inches (71.1 cm) of tan #4 silk cord

69 inches (1.8 m) of gold craft wire

Tools

Wire cutters

Chain-nose pliers

Round-nose pliers

Scissors

Crimping pliers

Finished Length

20 inches (50.8 cm)

Shaman Necklace

5 Use the 5-inch (12.7 cm) piece of wire to make a wrapped loop at one end that connects to the last loop of the beaded link chain. String on the focal bead. Make another wrapped loop to secure the focal bead.

6 Repeat step 3, starting the new chain by connecting to the open loop of the focal bead. Set the beaded chain aside.

Knotting the beads

7 Cut the silk cord into two 14-inch (35.6 cm) pieces.

8 Use one of the cords to string on one crimp tube. Pass the cord through the last wrapped loop at one end of the beaded chain and back through the crimp tube, leaving a 1-inch (2.5 cm) tail. Crimp the tube with the crimping pliers (see page 21).

9 String on one 2 mm bead, one tiger ebony round bead, and one 2 mm bead. Snug the beads against the crimp and make an overhand knot (see page 25) close to the last bead strung. Make another overhand knot 3/8 inch (9.0 mm) from the first knot.

10 String on one 2 mm bead, one tiger ebony cube bead, and one 2 mm bead. Snug the beads against the last knot and make another knot close to the last bead strung. Make another overhand knot 3/4 inch (1.9 cm) from the last knot. Repeat this step once more.

11 String on one 2 mm bead, one tiger ebony round bead, and one 2 mm bead. Snug the beads against the crimp and make a square knot (see page 25) close to the last bead strung. Trim the thread close to the knot.

12 Close one knot cup over the last knot made.

13 Repeat steps 8 to 12 for the other side of the necklace.

Adding the Clasp

14 Connect one half of the clasp to one of the knot cups using the split ring. Repeat for the other half of the necklace.

Ocean Air Necklace

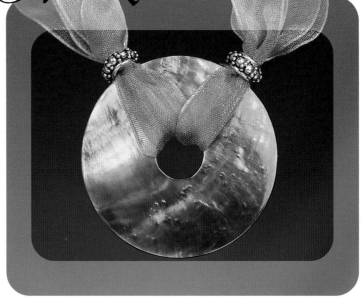

Light as air, but cool as the ocean, this easy-to-make piece designed by Jean Campbell is an unusual style of princess-length necklace. Change the focal donut bead to glass, resin, stone, or wood and modify the ribbon type, and you've got a whole new look.

Materials

1 mother-of-pearl 40 mm shell donut focal bead

9 Thai silver 5 mm x 8 mm wide-holed beads with a design

8 sterling silver 3 mm x 8 mm Bali-style wide-holed beads

2 sterling silver 4 mm seamless round beads

8 Thai silver 3 mm wide-holed faceted cube beads

2 sterling silver 15 mm x 34 mm Bali-style cones

1 sterling silver 26 mm S clasp to match the cones

7 feet (2.1 m) of ½-inch (1.3 cm) organza ribbon

6 inches of 20-gauge sterling silver wire

Tools

Wire cutters

Chain-nose pliers

Round-nose pliers

Scissors

Finished Length

18½ inches (47.0 cm)

Preparing the Components

1 Use the wire cutters to cut the sterling silver wire into two 3-inch (7.6 cm) pieces.

2 Use the chain- and round-nose pliers to form a 1/4-inch (6.0 mm) wrapped loop (see page 21) at one end of each wire. Set them aside.

3 Cut the ribbon into four equal lengths. Set them aside.

Stringing the Necklace

4 Take two of the ribbon lengths, even their ends, and pass them through the donut bead. Let the donut slide to the center of the ribbons and fold the ribbons in half.

5 Pair all four ribbon ends and string on one 3 mm x 8 mm bead. Slide the bead down to the donut to secure the ribbon in place. Repeat to add the remaining two ribbons to the donut.

6 Separate the ribbons. Randomly string on the remaining 3 mm x 8 mm beads and 5 mm x 8 mm beads. Place the beads so they are staggered through the length of the straps.

Completing the Necklace

7 Use one set of ribbons to tie a loose overhand knot (see page 25) onto one of the wrapped loops. Repeat for the other ribbons and wrapped loop. Adjust the

knots so each side of the necklace is even, leaving 2-inch (5.1 cm) tails. Tighten the knots.

8 String on one cone, from inside to outside, on one of the wrapped loop wires. String on one 4 mm round bead.

9 Tighten the cone and bead against the wrapped loop and use the chain- and round-nose pliers to make a wrapped loop that attaches to one half of the S clasp.

10 Repeat steps 8 and 9 to place a cone on the other side of the necklace.

11 String on one faceted cube bead on each of the exposed ribbon ends. Trim the ribbon ends at an angle.

Jupiter Circus Necklace

This colorful necklace designed by Mike Sherman evokes a stellar circus tent! Rich with stones and ornate gems, it will certainly take center ring.

Stringing the Necklace Straps

1. Cut six 16-inch (40.6 cm) and three 12-inch (30.9 cm) pieces of the beading wire.

2. Use one of the 16-inch (40.6 cm) pieces of wire to string on one crimp tube and the bar half of the clasp. Pass the wire back through the crimp tube leaving a 1-inch (2.5 cm) tail. Snug the tube and crimp (see page 21). Trim the wire close to the tube.

3. String on ten round beads. String on a sequence of one kyanite bead, one round bead, one chalcedony bead, and one round bead. Repeat the sequence. String on one kyanite bead, one round bead, one crimp tube, and the focal bead. Pass the wire back through the crimp tube. Slightly snug the beads, keeping a fairly loose loop around the focal bead. Crimp the tube. Trim any excess wire.

Materials

1 orange, yellow, and blue 48 mm lamp-worked donut focal bead

3 fire opal 53 mm flat coin beads

32 blue kyanite 12 mm x 37 mm flat oval beads

12 chalcedony 10 mm x 20 mm faceted flat drum beads

76 jade ~10 mm nugget beads

97 fire opal 8 mm round beads

18 sterling silver 2 mm x 2 mm crimp tubes

1 sterling silver 10 mm x 32 mm toggle clasp with an Australian opal inset

20 feet (6.1 m) of yellow .019 flexible beading wire

Tools

Wire cutters

Crimping pliers

2 bead clips

Finished Length

28 inches (71.1 cm)

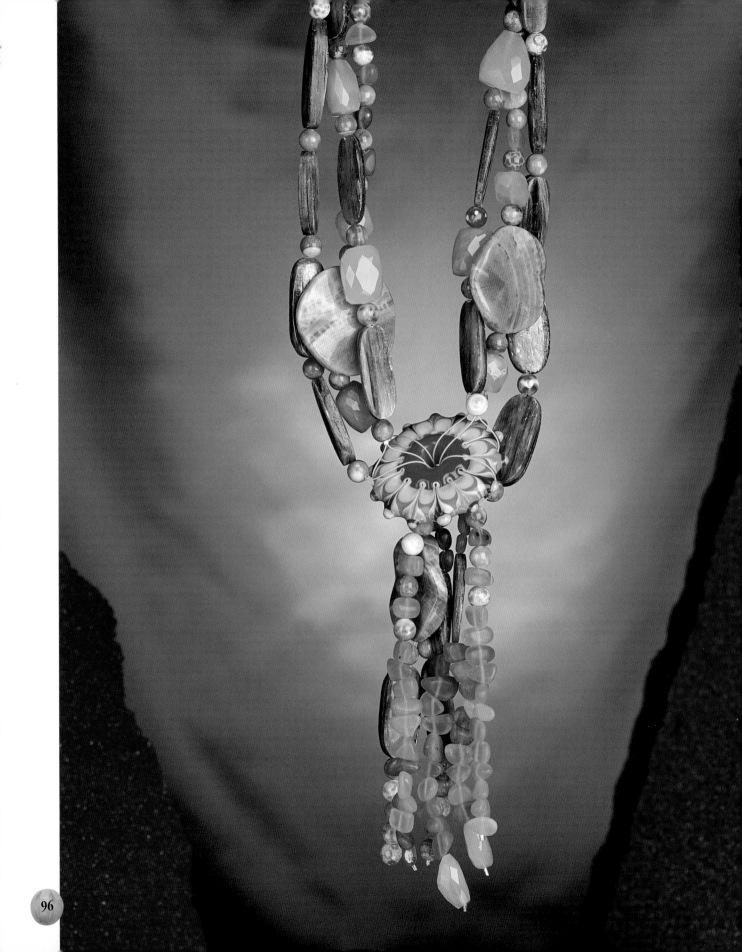

Jupiter Circus Necklace

4 Repeat step 2, adding the wire to the right side of the one you placed in step 3.

5 String on a sequence of one jade bead and one round bead. Repeat the sequence nine times. String on one chalcedony bead, one round bead, one coin bead, one round bead, one chalcedony bead, one round bead, and one crimp tube. Pass the wire through the center of the focal bead to the right of the strand you placed in step 3. Pass the wire back through the crimp tube. Slightly snug the beads so the loops from step 3 and this step are the same size. Crimp the tube. Trim any excess wire.

6 Repeat step 2, adding the wire to the left side of the one you placed in step 3.

7 String on five round beads, one chalcedony bead, and one round bead. String on a sequence of one kyanite bead and one round bead. Repeat the sequence four more times. String on one crimp tube. Pass the wire through the center of the focal bead to the left of the strand you placed in step 3. Pass the wire back through the crimp tube. Slightly snug the beads so the loops around the focal bead are all the same size. Crimp the tube. Trim any excess wire.

8 Repeat steps 2 to 7 for the ring side of the clasp, this time placing the strands so they mirror the other half of the necklace.

Stringing the Fringe

9 Working on the back of the focal bead, pass one of the 12-inch (30.9 cm) pieces of wire through the center three loops on the focal bead. String one round bead on each wire end. Pair the wire ends and string on one round bead and one coin bead. Place a clip on one of the wire ends. On the other end of the wire, string on one round bead, one kyanite bead, five round beads, and one crimp tube. Place a clip on this end of the wire. Remove the clip on the other wire end and string on one round bead, one kyanite bead, five round beads, and one crimp tube. Place a clip on this end of the wire. Even the wires, remove the clips, and crimp the tubes. Trim any excess wire.

10 Working on the back of the focal bead, pass one of the 12-inch (30.9 cm) pieces of wire through the second and fifth loops on the focal bead. Place a clip on one end of the wire. On the other end, string on one round bead, three jade beads, one kyanite bead, ten jade beads, one chalcedony bead, and one crimp tube. Slide the tube to the end of the wire and crimp the tube. Remove the clip on the other end of the wire and repeat the stringing sequence. Crimp the tube and trim any excess wire.

11 Working on the back of the focal bead, pass the last 12-inch (30.9 cm) piece of wire through the first and sixth loops on the focal bead. Place a clip on one end of the wire. On the other end, string on a sequence of one jade bead and one round bead. Repeat the sequence two more times. String on twelve jade beads and one crimp tube. Slide the tube to the end of the wire and crimp the tube. Remove the clip on the other end of the wire and repeat the whole stringing sequence. Crimp the tube and trim any excess wire.

Magic Trails Lariat

Materials

1 black and ivory 24 mm x 50 mm printed domino focal bead

3 black 12 mm x 14mm oval beads

4 black 12 mm x 13 mm pressed glass top-drilled flat triangles

1 African brass 12 mm round bead with striations

2 black 10 mm flat round beads

6 black 7 mm pressed glass dimpled round beads

1 sterling silver 6 mm seamless round bead

8 Thai silver 6 mm faceted cube beads

1 white 5 mm x 12 mm bone saucer bead

6 Thai silver 5 mm x 7 mm rondelle beads with a stamped design

7 Thai silver 4 mm x 9 mm triangle beads with a stamped design

1 white 4 mm x 9mm bone rondelle bead

31 sterling silver 4 mm seamless round beads

18 white 3 mm x 6 mm bone saucer beads

8 sterling silver 3 mm seamless round beads

64 sterling silver 2 mm seamless round beads

1 tube of beige size 11° hex-cut seed beads

1 tube of black size 8° seed beads

2 beige 15 mm 2-holed buttons

1 beige 20mm 2-holed button

1 beige 23 mm 4-holed button

1 beige 26 mm 2-holed button

13 sterling silver 2 mm x 2mm crimp tubes

3 sterling silver 2-inch (5.1 cm) head pins

1 sterling silver 6 mm soldered jump ring

1 sterling silver 5 mm split ring

1 sterling silver 13 mm hook clasp

60 inches (1.5 m) of .014-inch (.036 cm) flexible beading wire

This piece by Jean Campbell illustrates that a lariat-style necklace is a great way to show off an unusual top-drilled bead. Adding buttons and a wide variety of beads makes this asymmetrical design pure magic.

Tools

Wire cutters

Bead clip

Crimping pliers

Chain-nose pliers

Round-nose pliers

Finished Length

28 inches (71.1 cm)

Attaching the Focal Bead

1 Cut a 13-inch (33 cm) length of the beading wire with the wire cutters. Pass the end of the wire through the focal bead. String on a sequence of one 2 mm bead and one size 11° bead. Repeat the sequence four more times. Clip the end of the wire. Repeat the sequence five times on the other end of the wire.

Magic Trails Lariat

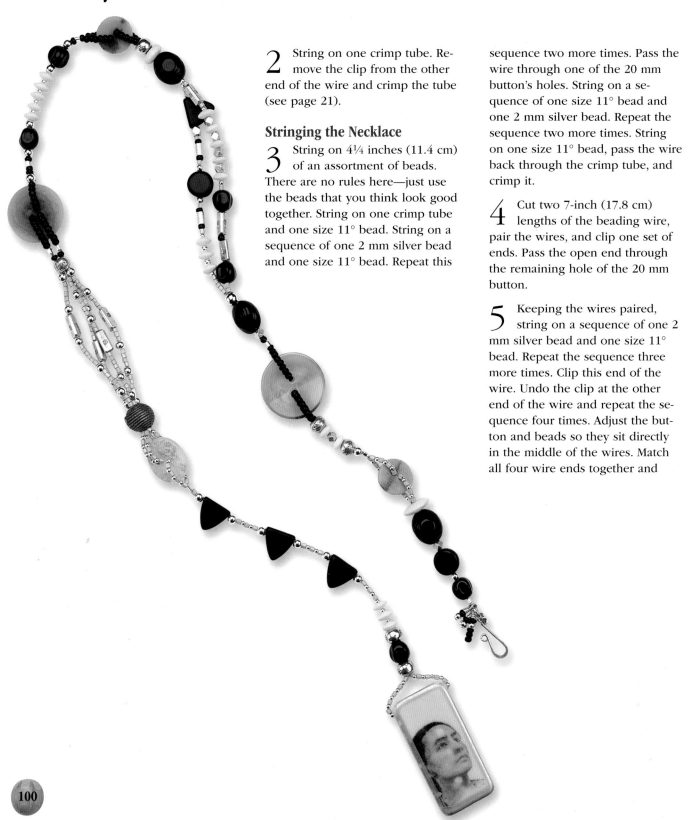

2 String on one crimp tube. Remove the clip from the other end of the wire and crimp the tube (see page 21).

Stringing the Necklace

3 String on 4¼ inches (11.4 cm) of an assortment of beads. There are no rules here—just use the beads that you think look good together. String on one crimp tube and one size 11° bead. String on a sequence of one 2 mm silver bead and one size 11° bead. Repeat this sequence two more times. Pass the wire through one of the 20 mm button's holes. String on a sequence of one size 11° bead and one 2 mm silver bead. Repeat the sequence two more times. String on one size 11° bead, pass the wire back through the crimp tube, and crimp it.

4 Cut two 7-inch (17.8 cm) lengths of the beading wire, pair the wires, and clip one set of ends. Pass the open end through the remaining hole of the 20 mm button.

5 Keeping the wires paired, string on a sequence of one 2 mm silver bead and one size 11° bead. Repeat the sequence three more times. Clip this end of the wire. Undo the clip at the other end of the wire and repeat the sequence four times. Adjust the button and beads so they sit directly in the middle of the wires. Match all four wire ends together and

string on one crimp tube. Snug the beads and crimp the tube. String on the African brass bead and slide it down over the crimp tube.

6 Separate the wires and string on 2¼ inches (5.7 cm) of assorted beads on each one.

7 Pair two of the wires and string on one size 8° bead, one crimp tube, and seven size 8° beads. Pass the wires through a hole in the 23 mm button. String on seven size 8° beads. Pass the wires through the crimp tube, snug the beads, and crimp the tube. Repeat this step for the remaining two wires, passing them through an adjacent button hole.

8 Cut 6 inches (15.2 cm) of the beading wire and pass the end through one of the remaining holes of the 23 mm button. String on six size 8° beads, one 3 mm silver bead, one size 8° bead, and one crimp tube, leaving a 1-inch (2.5 cm) tail. Clip this end of the wire. At the other end of the wire, string on six size 8° beads and one 3 mm silver bead. Pass the wire end through the last size 8° bead and crimp tube strung on the other wire end. Undo the clip. Snug the beads and crimp the tube.

9 String on 2 inches (5.1 cm) of assorted beads. Use size 8° beads and a crimp tube to attach the wire end to one hole of the 15 mm button, as you did in step 8.

10 Cut 10 inches (25.4 cm) of the beading wire. Pass it through the remaining hole of the button you last placed. String on five size 8° beads on one end of the wire and five on the other. Pair the wire ends and string on one crimp tube. Snug the beads and crimp the tube.

11 Keeping the wires paired, string on one Thai silver rondelle to cover the crimp tube and two other accent beads. Separate the wires and string on 3½ inches (8.9 cm) of assorted beads. Pair the wires again and string on three assorted beads, one size 8° bead, one crimp tube, and eight size 8° beads. Pass the wires through a hole of the 26 mm button.

12 String on seven size 8° beads. Pass the wires through the last size 8 bead strung in step 11 and the crimp tube. Snug the beads and crimp the tube.

13 Cut 5 inches (12.7 cm) of beading wire. In the same manner as you did in step 8, connect the 26 mm button and a 15 mm button. This time use size 8° beads to make the large button connection and a 2 mm silver bead/size 11° bead sequence on the small one. For the center section, only string on 1 inch (2.5 cm) of assorted beads.

14 Repeat step 13, this time connecting the remaining hole of the small button to the soldered jump ring, and stringing on 1½ inches (3.8 cm) of assorted beads. Set the lariat aside.

Making the Dangles

15 Use one head pin to string on an assortment of size 8° beads and one 3 mm silver bead. Use the chain- and round-nose pliers to make a wrapped loop (see page 21) to secure the beads. Repeat to make three dangles in all. Set them aside.

Finishing the Necklace

16 Use the split ring to connect the hook clasp, all of the dangles, and the soldered jump ring to the end of the lariat.

Pink Flame Necklace

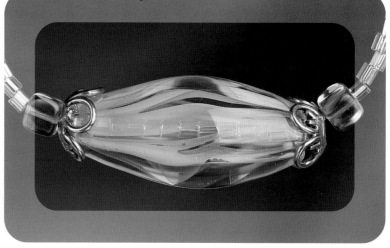

The flame that helped create this focal bead seems to be captured within. In this design, the bead is held at the throat by one delicate strand of accent and seed beads.

Materials

1 transparent pink 17 mm x 40 mm lampworked borosilicate glass focal bead

4 transparent pink 7 mm x 9 mm faceted cube beads

2 transparent pink 5 mm cube beads

4 sterling silver 5 mm x 7 mm rondelles

1 tube of transparent pink size 8° hex-cut seed beads

2 sterling silver 7 mm x 12 mm filigree bead caps (or sized to fit the focal bead)

2 sterling silver 10 mm x 18 mm cones with a floral design

1 sterling silver 20 mm S clasp with a floral design

22 inches (55.9 cm) of .014-inch (.036 cm) flexible beading wire

6 inches of 20-gauge sterling silver wire

Tools

Wire cutters

Chain-nose pliers

Round-nose pliers

2 bead clips

Finished Length

16½ inches (41.9 cm)

Preparing the Components

1 Use the wire cutters to cut the sterling silver wire into two 3-inch (7.6 cm) pieces.

2 Use the chain- and round-nose pliers to form a wrapped loop (see page 21) at one end of each wire. Set them aside.

Stringing the Beads

3 Place a clip 3 inches (7.6 cm) from one end of the flexible beading wire. String on one 7 mm x 9 mm bead, 33 seed beads, one silver rondelle, one 7 mm x 9 mm bead, one silver rondelle, 15 seed beads, and one cube bead.

4 String on one bead cap from the outside in, the focal bead, and one bead cap from the inside out. *Note:* A nice touch with transparent focal beads is to add seed

Pink Flame Necklace

beads within the bead hole. To do this, add the seed beads to the strand before you add the second bead cap.

5 Repeat step 3 in reverse. Place a clip on this end of the strand.

6 Check the design and make any adjustments. Make sure there is an equal amount of bare beading wire on each side of the strand.

Completing the Core Strand

7 Remove the clip from one end of the strand. Use a figure-eight knot (see page 25) to tightly tie one end of the beading wire to one of the wrapped loops. Snug the beads and repeat to attach the other end of the necklace to the second wrapped loop. If possible, pass the beading wire back through the beads on the strand. Trim any excess beading wire.

8 String on one cone, from inside to outside, on one of the wrapped loop wires.

9 Tighten the cone against the beadwork and use the chain- and round-nose pliers to make a wrapped loop that attaches to one half of the S clasp (see Making a Core Strand, page 23).

10 Repeat steps 8 and 9 to complete the other side of the necklace.

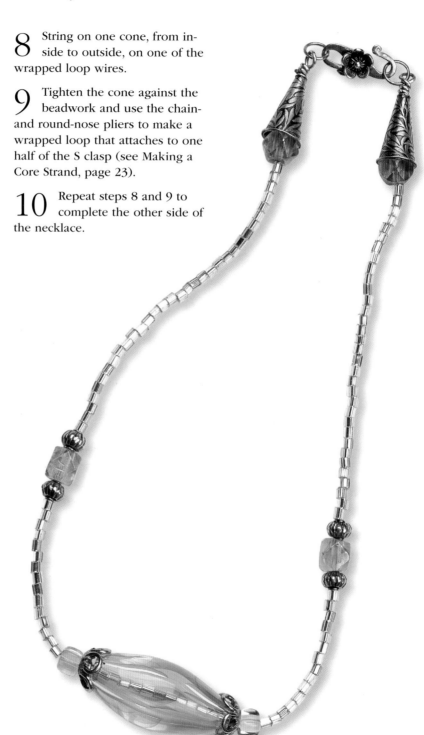

Gallery

Right: Kristy Wallington Nijenkamp
Wilma Flintstone's Pink BamBam, 2006
Necklace: 18 inches (45.7 cm)
Focal bead: 1 x 1 inch (2.8 x 2.5 cm)
Glass lampwork focal beads, rose quartz,
sterling silver spacers; stringing
Photo by artist

Below: Margie Deeb
Chaos Necklace, 1999
12 x 3 x ½ inches (30.5 x 7.6 x 1.3 cm)
Fused glass, seed beads, dichroic beads
Photo by artist

Top left: Lisa Niven Kelly
My Three Loves, 1999
Necklace: 24 inches (61 cm)
Focal bead: 4 x 2 inches (10.2 x 5.1 cm)
Seed beads, wirework, glass beads
Photo by Mindy Procsi

Top right: Margie Deeb
Untitled, 2003
9 x 3 x 1 inches (22.9 x 7.6 x 2.5 cm)
Seed beads, zephyr glass beads; tubular herringbone stitch
Photo by artist

Left: Diane Fitzgerald
Just a Rose, 1998
Focal bead by Angela Green
Necklace: ⅝ x 24 inches (1.6 x 61 cm)
Focal bead: 1¼ x 1¼ inches (3 x 3 cm)
Crystal chips; open netting
Photo by artist

Top: Nancy Kugel
Coffee Break Necklace and Earrings, 2006
Focal bead by Melanie Brooks-Lukacs
Necklace: 25 inches (63.5 cm)
Focal bead: 1½ x 1½ inches (3.8 x 3.8 cm)
Coffee pot focal beads, Czech glass; stringing
Photo by Bill Lemke

Top right: Kristy Wallington Nijenkamp
Pearls of Golden Green Dreams, 2006
Necklace: 18 inches (45.7 cm)
Focal bead: ¹¹⁄₁₆ x 1 inch (1.8 x 2.8 cm)
Glass lampwork focal bead, pearls, sterling silver
beads; stringing
Photo by artist

Right: Candice Wakumoto
Kake Hana Hou, 2003
Necklace: 18 inches (45.7 cm)
Focal bead: 1½ x 1½ inches (3.8 x 3.8 cm)
Silver clay, pear cut garnet, citrines, freshwater
pearls, garnets, sterling silver, handformed silver
clay, hand fabricated bezel with hand set gemstone
Photo by Larry Sanders

Christi Friesen
Festival Day, 2006
11 x 7 x 1½ inches (27.9 x 17.8 x 3.8 cm)
Mixed media, polymer clay, semiprecious stone
beads, pearls
Photo by artist

Elizabeth Ann Scarborough
Maggie Brown's Garden Necklace, 2005
Focal bead by Mavis Smith
20 inches (50.8 cm)
Bali silver clasp, pressed glass leaves, flowers,
drops, Venetian beads, lampwork beads
Photo by artist

Top left: Jean Campbell
Riot of Spring, 2005
18 inches (45.7 cm)
Rose quartz, Czech pressed-glass, Peruvian ceramic,
seed beads; stringing
Photo by Margie Deeb

Top right: Nancy Kugel
Koi Passthru, 2004
Necklace: 28 inches (71.1 cm)
Focal bead: 1 x 1 inch (2.5 x 2.5 cm)
Ne'Qua technique
Photo by Bill Lemke

Right: Bernard A. Superfine
Tagua Nut Squash Blossom, 2007
15 x 7 x ¾ inches (38.1 x 17.8 x 1.9 cm)
Tagua nuts, hemp, turquoise beads; macramé
Photo by Dick Kaplan

Acknowledgments

Many thanks to my husband Bob and my daughters Ciana and Siobhan, who with good grace live in a house with beads on the table, in the kitchen, under the sofa cushions, on the shelves—in short, everywhere. Especially Bob, who never for a second doubted that I could write a book, who took pictures for me at a moment's notice, and never complained about all late nights I spent at the computer. This book is for you.

To my teacher, Elizabeth Knodle, who taught me all about focal beads and how to bead with them. Without her generous encouragement, this book would not have been possible.

To Jean Campbell, my editor, who counted everything twice and provided laughs along the way, and then went above and beyond the call of duty to provide beautiful projects for the book.

To all my beading and jewelry friends in Dallas, who inspire me with their creativity: Martha Ann Reading, Ann Davis, Martha Puckett, Petey Ann Connolly, Bementa Ingalls, and others too numerous to mention … you know who you are.

To all the wonderful bead artists out there including those who are featured in this book: Anne Choi and the Karen Hill tribe (Lapis Queen, 34), Susan Pickle (Mandala Mix, 37), Susan Simonds (High Tea, 40 and Dancer's Song, 80), Bronwen Heilman (Verdant Spirals, 43 and Vienna Waltz, 57), Karen Lorraine (Tightrope Walker, 46), John Curtis (Spring Buds, 51), Klew (Carnival Jungle, 54), Nikki Blanchard (Ancient Forest, 60), Ann Campbell (Ella's Voice, 63), Andrea Guarino (Mardi Gras, 68 and Eclectique, 83), Sachiko Kawakita (Iris Rhapsody, 72), Bill Irvine (Sakura, 75), Norma Brink (Wavy Sea, 78), Catherine Steele (Nonpareil, 86), Lillypilly (Shaman, 89), and Steve Rhoades (Pink Flame, 102). Thanks for making such wonderful beads for us all to enjoy. And to all you beaders out there, both mild and bold, if you're actually reading the acknowledgments, you deserve thanks too.

And finally, thanks to the nice people at Lark Books, who gave me this wonderful opportunity.

About the Designers

Jean Campbell is a craft author, editor, and teacher whose specialty is beading. She is the founding editor of *Beadwork* magazine, and has written several books, most recently *The New Beader's Companion*, *Getting Started Stringing Beads*, and *Beaded Weddings*. She has appeared on the DIY *Jewelry Making* show, *The Shay Pendray Show*, and PBS' *Beads, Baubles, and Jewels*. Jean lives in Minneapolis, Minnesota.

Lora LeFhae has been creating jewelry for about five years, first inspired by Lillypilly shell pendants. "I find it so incredibly relaxing; it clears my mind and rejuvenates me. Beads are just impossible to resist: once you fall in love with them there's no turning back."

Mike Sherman, owner of the Soft Flex Company, is a top-notch designer who thinks outside the box. He sets no limits or boundaries for his work, mixing unusual colors and shapes to create exquisite jewelry. Mike can be reached at info@softflexcompany.com.

About the Author

Sarah McConnell has been a bead artist and teacher for over a decade, and finds herself completely infatuated with focal beads. She has been a long-standing member of the Dallas Craft Guild and has studied extensively with master craftswoman Elizabeth Knodle.

Sarah has a background in watercolor painting, which has contributed greatly to her attention to color and design in her jewelry-making. She is also a certified PMC instructor, and she has tried her hand at all kinds of bead-making, including lampwork and Japanese washi (paper) beads. Her work is sold in many galleries throughout the United States. She lives in Lakeside, Montana, with her husband and two daughters. You may contact her at sarah@bigskybeads.com.

Index